WINNING THE RACE

by Cherie Noel

PositiveAction
BIBLE CURRICULUM

Winning the Race – Student Manual

First Edition by Cherie Noel

positiveaction.org

Fourth Edition, 2020
Third Printing, 2024
Printed in the United States of America
ISBN: 978-1-59557-341-4

Fourth Edition Writing and Revision
Christa Lord

Editing and Development
Jim Lord

Illustration
Del Thompson

Consulting and Contributions
Helen Boen, C.J. Harris, Nathan Hess, Kristi Houser, Duncan Johnson, Stephanie Smith, Reta Tomkowiak

Additional Graphics and Design
Shannon Brown, Christa Lord, Jim Lord, Jennie Miller, Jesse Snow

Map imagery derived from maps copyright © 2019, Map Resources.

Published by

Contents

Vocabulary

- **Prophet** – Someone who shares a spiritual message

- **Scripture** – Sacred writings; another name for the Bible

- **Testament** – A promise or record; the name for the two major divisions of books in the Bible

- **Gospel** – "Good news" or teaching about Jesus

- **Epistle** – A letter; one of the 21 letters in the New Testament

- **Tabernacle** – In Scripture, a tent compound where God showed His presence to Israel

- **Atonement** – When something wrong is erased or canceled

1-A Overview of the Bible

The Bible was written down by different authors over a period of 1,600 years. The writers came from many different backgrounds. Some were poets, teachers, singers, kings, fishers, and **prophets**. They wrote in at least three languages: Hebrew, Aramaic, and Greek.

God worked through these writers to record His Word for us. In the Bible, God has given us history, prophecy, stories, sermons, letters, and even poetry. All of this **Scripture** teaches us about God.

▶ Turn to the table of contents in your Bible and complete the following statements.

- ◉ The Bible has two main sections: the Old _________________________________ and the New.

- ◉ There are a total of __________ books in the Bible.

- ◉ The *first* book is called _____________________.

- ◉ The *last* book is called _______________________.

► Continue using the table of contents to write the missing books below.

The Old Testament	
Genesis	The Law
	The Law
Leviticus	The Law
Numbers	The Law
Deuteronomy	The Law
Joshua	History
Judges	History
	History
1 & 2 Samuel	History
1 & 2 Kings	History
1 & 2 Chronicles	History
Ezra	History
Nehemiah	History
Esther	History
Job	Wisdom / Poetry
	Wisdom / Poetry
Proverbs	Wisdom / Poetry
Ecclesiastes	Wisdom / Poetry
Song of Songs / Song of Solomon	Wisdom / Poetry
Isaiah	Major Prophets
Jeremiah	Major Prophets
Lamentations	Major Prophets
Ezekiel	Major Prophets
	Major Prophets
Hosea	Minor Prophets
Joel	Minor Prophets
	Minor Prophets
Obadiah	Minor Prophets
Jonah	Minor Prophets
Micah	Minor Prophets
Nahum	Minor Prophets
Habakkuk	Minor Prophets
Zephaniah	Minor Prophets
Haggai	Minor Prophets
Zechariah	Minor Prophets
	Minor Prophets

The New Testament	
Matthew	Gospels
Mark	Gospels
	Gospels
John	Gospels
	History
Romans	Letters / Epistles
1 & 2 Corinthians	Letters / Epistles
	Letters / Epistles
Ephesians	Letters / Epistles
Philippians	Letters / Epistles
Colossians	Letters / Epistles
1 & 2 Thessalonians	Letters / Epistles
1 & 2 Timothy	Letters / Epistles
Titus	Letters / Epistles
Philemon	Letters / Epistles
Hebrews	Letters / Epistles
	Letters / Epistles
	Letters / Epistles
1, 2, & 3 John	Letters / Epistles
Jude	Letters / Epistles
	Prophecy

1-B One Author, One Message

Even though the Bible was written down by many different types of people, it has one true Author in God Himself. The books of the Bible seem very different, but they all support one unified message.

▶ Read **2 Peter 1:19–21** and answer the following questions.

- ◉ Since God's prophecy is like a light in the dark, what should we do? (v. 19)

____

- ◉ If Scripture didn't come from people's imaginations, how *did* it come to us? (v. 21)

____

____

____

▶ Imagine that a friend asks you to explain what the Bible is about in just one sentence. What would you say?

____

____

____

▶ To answer this question better, let's see how God reached out to people throughout the Bible. Read the following verses and answer the questions.

Exodus 29:45–46	In the Old Testament, God told the people of Israel to build a **Tabernacle** so that He would live among them. What did God want them to know? ____________________ ____________________
Romans 3:20	God also gave Israel His Law. Because of this Law, what do we know about? ____________________
Leviticus 4:27–31	In the Old Testament, God gave people ways to show that they were sorry for their sin. If someone sinned but then offered the sacrifice God required, what would happen? ____________________ ____________________

So why don't Christians offer animal sacrifices today? Why don't we go to a Tabernacle to pray?

► Read **Ephesians 5:1–2** and answer the following questions.

⊙ Who should we follow and imitate? (v. 1) _________________________

⊙ What did Jesus Christ do for us? (v. 2)

____

____

Jesus died on a cross to take the punishment for our sin. He became the perfect sacrifice, and then He rose from the dead to show His power. He offers to forgive and save people who turn from their sin and follow Him. We don't need Old Testament rituals anymore.

When we read the Old and New Testaments together, we can understand the big message of the Bible. Scripture tells us how a perfect God loves sinful people like us. Because of Jesus' sacrifice, we can know God and be close to Him.

1-C Jesus the Word

All of Scripture points toward Jesus:

⊙ The Old Testament promises the coming of Jesus.

⊙ In the New Testament, the four Gospels record what He said and did before dying and rising again.

⊙ The Epistles explain how we can be like Him.

⊙ And the Book of Revelation promises that He'll come back one day.

Scripture is the *written* Word of God, and it shows us the *living* Word, who is Jesus. So there are two "Words" of God. We read one Word to know the other Word better.

► Read **John 1:1**. What three things does John say about the Word?

1. ____

2. ____

3. ____

► Continue reading in **John 1:2–18** and fill the blanks in the following summaries.

Verses 1–3	The Word was God, and everything was created by Him.
Verse 4	In the Word was ______________, which was the light of everyone.
Verse 10	The Word was in the world, but the people did not __________________ Him, even though He had made everything.
Verse 12	Those who received the Word became _____________________ of God.

► Look again at **John 1:14–17**. Which Word was John talking about in this chapter?

  ☐ The written Word   ☐ The living Word   ☐ Some other word

► If the Word is like a light to us, what do you think the "darkness" is?

____

► Finally, read **John 1:14** again, along with **Philippians 2:5–8**. What do you think John meant when he wrote about the Word becoming "flesh"?

____

____

Since Jesus is fully God and fully human, He is the perfect bridge between God and His people. As the living Word, Jesus brings us light and life. By studying Jesus, we can know God and enjoy His gifts better.

Winning Your Race

If you rely on the truth of God's Word, you can run your life's race well. No matter what challenges you face, God can be your strength.

► What is something you want to learn about Scripture this year?

____

____

____

► How do you want to change or grow?

____

____

____

LESSON 2
Seeking God's Word

Vocabulary

- **Wisdom** – The ability to use knowledge well; insight and understanding

- **Inspiration** – The way God worked through human writers to record Scripture; "God-breathed"

- **Doctrine** – An important teaching or belief, often by a religious group

- **Reproof / Rebuke** – To tell people that they have done wrong

- **Idolatry** – The practice of worshiping idols or false gods

- **Covenant** – A binding agreement between two or more people; a promise

2-A Pictures of the Word

We won't know God well unless we spend time learning His Word. Scripture tells us who God is and what He's like. He made us to know, love, and follow Him, but we cannot do these things well without the Bible. After all, if you love someone but never listen to what they say, do you really love them?

▶ The Bible helps us know God better in many ways. Match the passages below to their main ideas.

A. Psalm 19:7	B. Psalm 119:9–11	C. John 5:24, 37–40	D. 2 Timothy 3:16

	God's Law can help our soul and give us **wisdom**.
	Scripture points to Jesus, who offers us eternal life. To know God the Father, we must listen to His Word.
	God's Word helps us follow His commands and avoid sinning against Him.
	Scripture offers us good **doctrine** and corrects us from doing wrong.

▶ The writers of Scripture used many different pictures to explain how God uses His Word. Read the following passages and fill in the blanks. Then draw a picture of each thing that the Word is like.

Psalm 119:105–106	Matthew 13:8, 23
God's Word is like a __________________ that helps us walk along a dark path.	The Word is like a ________________ that grows in our heart to produce fruit.

Hebrews 4:12	James 1:22–25
God's Word is alive and sharper than a ______________________________. It cuts deep to show our inner self.	Hearing the Word is like seeing our face in a ________________________. It shows us what we should change.

▶ Think about all the passages you've read in this lesson so far. If you choose to study Scripture, how do you expect God to use His Word in your life?

____

____

____

____

____

2-B The Boy King

After the reign of King Solomon, the Israelites split into two separate kingdoms: Israel in the north and Judah in the south. The following years were a dark time for both kingdoms. The leaders and the people worshiped false gods and did horrible things to each other. There were no godly rulers in Israel and only a few in Judah.

One of the good kings of Judah was named Josiah. He became the king of Judah when he was only eight years old.

► Read about how Josiah became king in **2 Chronicles 33:1–6** and **21–25**.

⊙ What kind of king was Josiah's grandfather Manasseh? (vv. 1–6)

____

____

____

____

____

____

⊙ King Manasseh eventually turned from his evil ways and asked God for forgiveness. Did his son Amon do the same? (vv. 21–23) ☐ Yes ☐ No

⊙ Why did Josiah become king before he could grow up? (vv. 24–25)

____

____

This did not seem like a good start for Josiah. His father had not taught him about God. The land was filled with *idolatry* and other wickedness. The people had forgotten about God's Law. How could a child lead a nation like this?

► Josiah became a good leader for one reason—he decided to follow God. Read the following verses in **2 Chronicles 34** and mark the correct ending to each sentence.

Verses 1–3: In the eighth year of his reign, Josiah chose to seek . . .		
☐ allies from the nations around Judah.	☐ the approval of wealthy people in Jerusalem.	☐ the God of his ancestor, King David.

☐ build a new temple for God.

☐ destroy places where people worshiped idols.

☐ write a new book of Scripture.

☐ the wall around Jerusalem.

☐ the House (Temple) of the Lord in Jerusalem.

☐ the high places he had once torn down.

☐ an old loaf of bread.

☐ the robes worn by Aaron the priest.

☐ the Book of the Law of the Lord.

☐ tore his clothes in sorrow and anguish.

☐ jumped for joy.

☐ smashed his throne in anger.

When Josiah finally heard the Law of God, he was sad that his people had ignored it for so long. The Word of God changed Josiah and his kingdom.

2-C Josiah's Humility

In the Book of Deuteronomy, God told His people about all the blessings He would give them if they followed Him. He also explained the curses that would come on them if they rejected Him and worshiped false gods.

▶ Read **2 Chronicles 34:19–21**. After King Josiah heard God's Law, why was he distressed?

____

____

____

____

Josiah was humble enough to know that he needed help from God. He didn't try to ignore God and do whatever he wanted. Instead, he wanted to help Israel follow the ways of the Lord.

▶ Continue reading in **2 Chronicles 34:22–33** and fill in the blanks below.

Josiah told Hilkiah the priest to ask God for answers. So Hilkiah went to __________
verse 22
the prophetess. She gave Hilkiah two messages from God:

1. God would bring terrible things to Judah—including all the __________
verse 24
described in the Book of Deuteronomy. This would happen because the people had rejected God.

2. Because Josiah __________ himself before God, the Lord listened to
verse 27
him. The kingdom would not suffer as long as Josiah lived.

When Josiah heard God's message, he gathered everyone at the Temple and read all the words of the Book of the __________. Then the king himself made a
verse 30
__________ to obey God's commands, and he told everyone else do the same.
verse 31

From that point onward, Josiah led the people to follow their Lord. For the rest of the king's reign, the nation served God and respected His Word.

Winning Your Race

Godly leaders need humility. We must be willing to seek help when we need it, and we must be willing to serve others when they need it. We all depend on God, so no one is too big or important to help people.

▶ Describe one way you like to help others.

____

____

____

▶ Explain how you could do this in a way that leads people to thank God—and not just you.

____

____

____

____

Vocabulary

- **Revelation** – Something that is revealed or shown; God's communication to us

- **Doubt** – To distrust; a feeling of uncertainty or unbelief about something

- **Parable** – A story that pictures or illustrates a lesson

- **Vineyard** – A place for growing grapevines

3-A God Speaks to Moses

The Bible is God's *revelation* to us. He revealed His Word so we could know Him better. When we read through all this history, poetry, and prophecy, we should ask what it shows us about God.

Before Scripture was complete, people needed to listen to God in different ways. When God first spoke to Moses, He appeared in an unusual form.

▶ Read **Exodus 3:1–8** and answer the following questions.

⊙ Before hearing God call to him, what did Moses see? (vv. 2–4)

____

⊙ God told Moses to show respect in this place. What did Moses need to do? (v. 5)

____

⊙ The Lord had seen the suffering of His people. What would He do now? (v. 8)

____

____

Suddenly, at the age of 80, Moses had a mission from God. The Israelites had lived in Egypt for 430 years. They spent much of that time as slaves. But God had compassion on them, and He told Moses to lead the people out of Egypt to their own land.

▶ When God called him, Moses didn't think he was a good choice. How did God answer Moses' **doubts** and questions? Read the following passages and fill in the blanks of each summary.

	Moses' Doubt	God's Answer
Exodus 3:11–12	Who am I to go to Pharaoh and bring out the people?	I will be _______________________.
Exodus 3:13–14	What if they ask for the name of the God who sent me?	Say, "_______________ has sent me to you."
Exodus 4:1–5	But the people will not believe me or listen to me.	God turned Moses' _______________________ into a _______________________, and then changed it back again. This would be one sign of God's power.
Exodus 4:10–12	But I cannot speak well.	I will teach you what _______________________ _______________________.

▶ From this conversation, how do you think Moses felt about what God asked him to do?

____

▶ Finally, read **Exodus 4:13–20** and answer the following questions.

⊙ Who was sent by God to help Moses speak? (vv. 14–16) _______________

⊙ Did Moses eventually decide to go? (v. 20) ☐ Yes ☐ No

3-B God Speaks to Jonah

Many years after Moses led Israel out of Egypt, God spoke to Jonah the prophet. God didn't ask Jonah to help some poor, oppressed people. Instead, Jonah needed to share God's truth with Israel's enemies—the wicked, violent people of Nineveh.

▶ Read the following passages and match each sentence to its correct ending.

	Jonah 1:1–3 – When God first told Jonah to preach in Nineveh, Jonah . . .	**A.** got on a ship heading for Tarshish.
	Jonah 1:8–12 – When the sailors found out he was running from God, Jonah . . .	**B.** vomited Jonah up onto land.
	Jonah 1:16–17 – Before Jonah could drown, God . . .	**C.** went to preach in Nineveh.
	Jonah 2:1–2, 10 – After Jonah prayed for help, God spoke to the fish, which . . .	**D.** made a huge fish swallow him.
	Jonah 3:1–3 – The second time that God told Jonah to go to Nineveh, Jonah . . .	**E.** told them to throw him into the sea.

▶ Read all of **Jonah 4** and answer the following questions.

◉ When Jonah found out that God wouldn't destroy Nineveh after all, how did he feel? (vv. 1–4)

____

◉ What do you think God taught Jonah with the plant that died?

____

____

____

► Read each statement and mark if it applies to Moses or Jonah. Some statements may be true for both men or neither.

	Moses	Jonah
Chosen to help save the Israelites		
Chosen to help save the Ninevites		
Was afraid to do what God said to do		
Obeyed God's commands without doubt or hesitation		
Told God his doubts and fears		
Ran away from God's calling		
Eventually asked God for help		
Didn't want his audience to listen to him and change		

3-C True Obedience

► In **Matthew 21:28–32**, Jesus told a **parable** to some religious leaders who were very prideful. Read the story and mark the correct ending to each sentence.

Verses 28–29: In the story, the first son . . .

☐ worked in the **vineyard** as soon as he was told.
☐ said he wouldn't work, but later did, after all.
☐ said he wouldn't work and then relaxed all day.

Verse 30: When the second son was told to go work, he . . .

☐ worked in the vineyard as soon as he was told.
☐ said he wouldn't work, but later did, after all.
☐ said he would go to the vineyard, but did not.

Verse 31: The son who actually obeyed his father was . . .

☐ the first son.

☐ the second son.

☐ neither son.

Verse 32: Jesus showed the religious leaders that they were like . . .

☐ the first son.

☐ the second son.

☐ neither son.

The religious leaders claimed to obey God, but they didn't really. Jesus pointed to other kinds of sinners with bad reputations. He said that even these people could enter God's kingdom before prideful leaders.

Winning Your Race

God wants us to listen to His words and respond to them. It's not enough just to know about Scripture. We should learn *and* do. The Word can change us from the inside out.

▶ Look again at **James 1:22–25**. If we hear the Word but don't do what it says, who are we like?

____

____

The whole point of a mirror is to show you what you look like. Is your hair messed up? Do you have a smudge on your nose?

Scripture can do the same thing, but spiritually. The Word shows us who Jesus is. We can study Him and compare ourselves to His love and kindness.

▶ In the spaces below, list three reasons why it can be difficult to study God's Word.

⦿ _______________________________________

____

⦿ _______________________________________

____

⦿ _______________________________________

____

▶ Choose one of the reasons above and explain how you might make it *less* difficult. How can you seek help? How can you study the Word despite the challenge?

____

____

____

____

____

Designed for His Glory

Vocabulary

- **Glory** – The honor, praise, or credit for being great

- **Thresh** – To separate grain from the rest of the plant

- **Winepress** – In ancient times, a hard floor or pit where people squeezed grapes to make wine

- **Ba'al** – An Old Testament name for many local false gods; can mean "lord" or "ruler"

- **Fleece** – A coat of wool; often taken from sheep

4-A God Knows You

People are a lot alike, but no two are exactly the same. There's no one else in the world just like you.

► Think about yourself and complete the sentences below.

- I would describe myself as _______________________, _______________________, and _______________________.

- I enjoy _______________________, _______________________, and _______________________.

- I am good at _______________________ and _______________________.

- I struggle with _______________________ and _______________________.

- If I could change anything about myself, it would be _______________________ _______________________ _______________________.

God created humans in His image. This makes us different than everything else in the universe. Through God's Word, we can understand some of His thoughts and have a relationship with Him.

God wants us to know Him, but He already knows everything about us. He knows our likes and dislikes, what we're good at, and what makes us sad. He knew everything about each of us even before we were born.

► David wrote about God's knowledge and care in **Psalm 139**. Read the verses below and answer the questions.

⊙ What does God know about us? List at least three things from **verses 1–4**.

____

____

____

____

____

⊙ In **verses 13–16**, why does David praise God?

____

____

► It's difficult to be thankful for our struggles. The Apostle Paul struggled with many challenges. In **1 Corinthians 1:26–31**, he explains one reason why God does not immediately take away our weaknesses. Read the passage and complete the summaries below.

Verse 26	Paul tells the Corinthian believers that not many of them were _______________ _______________________________________.
Verse 27	But God chose foolish and weak things to _______________________ the wise and strong.
Verse 29	Why? So that no one could _______________________ in God's presence. God deserves all the credit and *glory* for everything good.
Verse 30	Because of God, we are in _______________________, who has become our wisdom and everything else we need to be close to God.

4-B God Calls Gideon

When the Israelites conquered Canaan around 1400 BC, God told them to remove all the idols from the land. The people chose not to do so, and soon they began to worship the idols.

Because of this, God allowed the nation of Midian to attack Israel. The Israelites suffered greatly, but they eventually turned and cried to God for help. God heard their pleas and prepared someone to rescue Israel from the Midianites.

This person's name was Gideon. Like many others in the Bible, he did not feel like he could do what God wanted him to do. But God still helped him and worked through him.

▶ Read **Judges 6:11–16** and answer the questions.

- The angel appeared while Gideon **threshed** wheat in a **winepress**. Even though Gideon was hiding, what did the angel call him? (v. 12)

  ____

- More importantly, who was with Gideon? (v. 12) ____

- Do you think Gideon believed the angel? ☐ Yes ☐ No

  Why or why not? ____

  ____

  ____

Gideon didn't think that he was the right person to help rescue Israel, but God promised to be with him as he defeated the Midianites.

▶ Gideon still had doubts, but he looked to God for answers. Continue reading the following verses in **Judges 6** and complete the sentences.

Verse 17	Gideon asked for a ____________ that God was really talking to him. The angel touched Gideon's food with a staff, and it burned up like an offering. (vv. 19–21)
Verses 25–27	God told Gideon to tear down the ____________________________, build a new one for God, and then make an offering. Gideon obeyed.
Verses 36–38	Gideon asked God for another sign. He wanted his ____________________ to be wet with morning dew while the ground stayed dry. God gave him the sign.
Verses 39–40	Gideon wanted yet another sign. This time, the ____________________ would be *dry* while the rest of the ground stayed *wet*. Again, God answered his request.

4-C Gideon Trusts God

▶ Even before the battle with Midian, God gave Gideon a difficult lesson in trust. Read **Judges 7:1–8** and fill in the blanks.

Many men left their homes to join Gideon's new army. The Israelites camped by the spring of _______________ (verse 1) near the valley where the Midianites were. Then the Lord told _______________ (verse 2) that there were too _______________ (verse 2) in Israel's army. If God defeated Midian with all these soldiers, people in Israel would say that their own _______________ (verse 2) had saved them.

So God told Gideon to send home anyone who was _______________ (verse 3). At that time, _______________ (verse 3) of the people returned home, while _______________ (verse 3) remained.

Still, God said that there were too many left. God told Gideon to bring the army to the spring to drink. Gideon needed to send home every soldier that knelt down at the water. He could keep the soldiers that stayed alert and _______________ (verse 6) water out of their hands. After this final test, Gideon had only _______________ (verse 7) men left.

▶ Continue reading in **Judges 7:9–25** and mark the correct endings to the following sentences.

☐ the house of Purah.   ☐ the camp of the enemy.   ☐ the Tabernacle.

☐ too many people and camels to even count.   ☐ a thousand soldiers.   ☐ twenty men and a crazed camel.

☐ some barley bread knocking over a tent.   ☐ a giant statue crumbling to the ground.   ☐ going into battle without his sword and shield.

☐ attacking the armies of Midian all by himself.   ☐ going home and waiting for the war to be over.   ☐ telling the army that God had already defeated Midian.

| ☐ swords, shields, and helmets. | ☐ trumpets, torches, and jars. | ☐ a great feast. |

| ☐ drew their swords and charged the enemy. | ☐ fired a volley of arrows, then dove behind cover. | ☐ blew the trumpets, broke the jars, and shouted all at once. |

| ☐ attacking each other and running away. | ☐ hiding in their tents. | ☐ launching a counterattack. |

| ☐ worshiped God and returned to their homes. | ☐ made Gideon their king. | ☐ chased the Midianites, killed their leaders, and took back the land. |

Winning Your Race

▶ Is it possible to have courage and fear at the same time? Why or why not?

____

____

____

____

▶ Imagine that your friend tries to do something difficult for God's glory but doesn't succeed at the task. How would you encourage this person?

____

____

____

____

____

____

____

____

LESSON 5
God's Purpose for Me

Vocabulary

- **Glorify** - To give honor and praise to someone; in Scripture, to point toward God's glory

- **Abound** – To increase, fill, and overflow

- **Exalt** – To lift higher; to call attention to

- **Disciple** – A student or follower who learns from a teacher

- **Conform** – To become like something or someone

- **Sanctify** – To make holy or sacred; to set apart for a special purpose

5-A Glorifying God

Gideon served God by helping rescue the people of Israel from the Midianites. Gideon obeyed God's call, and God received all the glory from the battle. Christians today might not go to war like Gideon did, but we do have a similar purpose, goal, or mission.

▶ What purpose has God given all of us? Read **Philippians 1:9–11** and complete the summaries.

Verse 9	Paul prayed that the believers' ________________ would **abound** more and more alongside their wisdom . . .
Verse 10	So that they could ________________ what is ________________ . . .
Verse 10	So they could be ________________ and ________________ until the day of Christ . . .
Verse 11	Filled with the ________________ of righteousness that comes through Jesus . . .
Verse 11	All to the glory and praise of ________________ .

The end of Philippians 1:11 explains why believers should grow in love, wisdom, and righteousness. God makes all of this happen to glorify Himself.

▶ What are some ways to glorify God? Read the following passages and match each to its primary message.

A.	B.	C.	D.	E.
Psalm 34:3	**Psalm 86:9**	**Matthew 5:16**	**Romans 1:21**	**Romans 4:16, 20–21**

	We should let our "light" shine so people can see the good we do and then glorify God.
	All nations will one day worship God and glorify His name.
	Abraham gave glory to God while having faith that God would keep His promise.
	We can glorify or magnify God by *exalting* His name.
	Some people do not recognize Him as God or show thanks to Him.

5-B Following Him

We can glorify God with our words, but we should also glorify God with our actions. By keeping God's commands, we honor Him. By showing love to other people, we point them to God's love. We can glorify God in everything good we do.

▶ Read what Jesus told His followers in **John 15:8–13** and then answer the questions below.

⊙ How is God the Father glorified? (v. 8)

____

____

⊙ Who is our example of obedience and love? (vv. 10–12) ____________________________

▶ We can follow God by learning from Jesus. Read what Paul wrote **Philippians 2:5–11** and complete the summaries.

Verse 5	We should have the same ________________________ that was in Jesus.
Verse 6	Jesus had the same form as God, but He did not use this for His own sake.
Verse 7	Instead, He took the form of a ________________________ and became human.
Verse 8	He ________________________ Himself and obeyed God, even to the point of death on a cross.

Verse 9	So God the Father has ___________________________ Jesus and has given Him a name above any other . . .
Verse 10	So that every ___________________ should bow at Jesus' name . . .
Verse 11	And so that every tongue say that Jesus Christ is ___________________, to the glory of God the Father.

Jesus is God, but He still humbled Himself, obeyed the Father, and took human form to save us. Everything Jesus did glorified God, and we should follow His example.

▶ Read **John 3:16–21**. Here Jesus explains God's plan to Nicodemus, a religious leader.

- Why did God the Father send His Son into the world? (v. 16)

  ____

  ____

- Who will have eternal life? (vv. 16–18)

  ____

- And if we walk in the light and truth of Jesus, who gets the glory for our good deeds? (v. 21)

  ____

5-C Just Like Jesus

▶ Read **Romans 8:28–29** and answer the following questions.

- What is God working all things toward? (v. 28)

  ____

  ____

- God has always known every person that would believe in His Son. Since before the beginning of time, He decreed that believers would be conformed to what? (v. 29)

  ____

Those who trust in Jesus Christ have found the path to God. As God leads us along this path, He **sanctifies** us and makes us more like Jesus. This is God's purpose for us. This is how we glorify Him.

What does God use to conform us to Christ? As we've studied in previous lessons, Scripture is the clearest picture of Jesus we have. We should study God's Word and wrestle with the truth we find there. But we don't have to learn everything all by ourselves. God has given us others to help.

► Read **Ephesians 4:11–14** and answer the following.

⊙ What kinds of people can help believers? (v. 11)

____

____

⊙ If we listen to wise, godly Christians and stay unified as a Christ-like church, what will we avoid? (v. 14)

____

____

Winning Your Race

If you have trusted Jesus Christ to save you, you are the heir to many gifts from God. You have a family of believers to help you, a library of Scripture to make you wise, and the promises of God Himself. He will work through you for your good and His glory.

► Name at least three people in your life who have helped you glorify God. Who has supported you, educated you, or challenged you?

⊙ ____

⊙ ____

⊙ ____

► Now think about a few specific people that *you* can help. How can you better show Christ to them? Take a moment to ask God for wisdom to help these people.

► Write one way you could glorify God in each of the following areas.

⊙ At home: _______________________________________

____

____

⊙ In your studies: _________________________________

____

____

⊙ With your church: ________________________________

____

LESSON 6
Filled with the Spirit

Vocabulary

- **Submit** – To serve someone or follow leadership; to put your wants under another's

- **The Flesh** – The part of us that wants to sin; our mortal weakness

- **Magistrate** – A government official that helps apply and enforce the law

6-A The Holy Spirit

Before Jesus went back to heaven, He prepared His disciples for when they could no longer see Him. In a way, He was leaving them behind. But at the same time, God would still be with them.

▶ Read what Jesus said in **John 14:15–17** and **25–29**. Then answer the following questions.

◉ Who would the Father send later? (v. 16) _______________________________

◉ What is another name for this Person? (vv. 17, 26) _______________________________

◉ Where would this Person live? (v. 17)

____

◉ What two big things would this Person do for Jesus' disciples? (v. 26)

  1. ____

  2. ____

◉ Why was Jesus telling His disciples that He would go away in a little while? (vv. 27–29)

____

____

____

Every person who trusts in Christ Jesus receives the Holy Spirit. The Spirit dwells in us and transforms our hearts. We can't make ourselves more Christ-like in our own power. We need God to be more godly.

Even though the Spirit works in us, He does not overrule our choices. We must still decide whether to follow the Spirit or to resist Him. If we choose to disobey God, the Spirit will show us that we have done wrong.

▶ Read **Ephesians 5:18** and write the two commands in this verse.

⊙ Don't ____

⊙ But rather be ____

▶ Paul contrasts these two things for a reason. What happens when someone drinks a lot of alcohol?

____

____

▶ So what happens when believers are filled with the Spirit? Keep reading in **Ephesians 5:18–21** and list the activities mentioned in these verses.

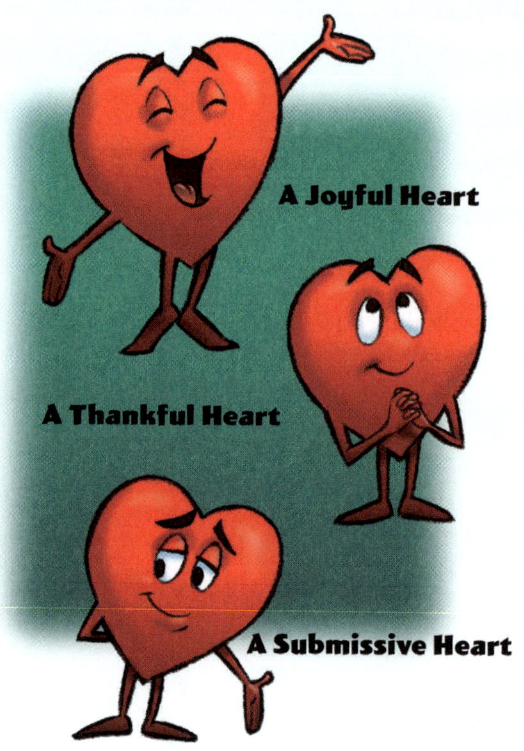

Verse 19	______________________ ______________________ ______________________ ______________________
Verse 20	______________________ ______________________
Verse 21	______________________ ______________________ ______________________ ______________________

To be filled with the Spirit, we must put ourselves completely under God's control. We must obey His commands, seek out His wisdom, and follow the example of Christ.

And we must say *no* to the desires that lead us into sin. When the Spirit fills us, He helps us grow and learn. But sin will harm us, distract us, and keep us from our true purpose.

6-B The Fruit of the Spirit

► Read what Paul wrote in **Galatians 5:16–21** and answer the following questions.

◉ If we walk with the Spirit, what will we *not* do? (v. 16)

____

◉ Paul describes a war inside us. What are the two sides of this conflict? (v. 17)

____

In verses 19–21, Paul lists a few of the many, many ways that the flesh can lead us into sin. There are too many to cover in this lesson, but all of them come from the same problem—doing what we want instead of what God wants.

► Continue reading in **Galatians 5:22–23**. Being careful to write them in order, list the fruit that the Spirit grows in us.

Trait	Description
1.	Choosing what is good for someone, no matter what
2.	Celebrating God's goodness; hopeful confidence in God's promises
3.	Resting in God's power and goodness in our lives
4.	The ability to endure troubles; waiting while trusting in God
5.	Love and tenderness shown to others
6.	Righteousness; moral behavior
7.	Loyal trust in God
8.	Humble care and grace shown to other people
9.	Training or disciplining ourselves to do right; keeping our "flesh" in check

As we walk with the Spirit, we will find this fruit in our lives. He alone can grow these things in us.

6-C Paul and Silas

When we face difficult times, others can see if we have the fruit of the Spirit. The missionaries Paul and Silas faced hardship in the city of Philippi, but they responded with love and joy.

▶ What did Paul and Silas do in Philippi? Read **Acts 16:16–34** and mark the following statements as true or false. Then write the numbers of the verses that helped you decide.

Statement	True or False?		Verses
Paul told the girl with the evil spirit to be quiet.	☐ True	☐ False	
Even though they had done nothing wrong, Paul and Silas were beaten and thrown into prison.	☐ True	☐ False	
While in prison, the missionaries wept and pleaded for mercy.	☐ True	☐ False	
During the earthquake, Paul and Silas escaped.	☐ True	☐ False	
When the jailer asked how he could be saved, Paul and Silas told him to set all the prisoners free.	☐ True	☐ False	
The jailer and his household believed in Christ and took care of the missionaries.	☐ True	☐ False	

▶ Before Paul and Silas told the jailer about Jesus, how did they show their trust in God?

____

____

____

____

Winning Your Race

▶ Read **Galatians 5:16–23** again. For each situation below, *write* or *draw* two responses. One response should be controlled by the flesh and the other by the Spirit.

Alton's teammate made fun of him during practice.	
Response in the Flesh	Response in the Spirit

Ana's parents said she had to stop watching videos and get ready for dinner.	
Response in the Flesh	Response in the Spirit

Miguel found out that his mom needs to have surgery.	
Response in the Flesh	Response in the Spirit

LESSON 7
Our Worship to God

Vocabulary

- **Rejoice** – To take joy from something good; in Scripture, to appreciate God's gifts

- **Favor** – Special blessings or grace; goodwill

7-A Praising God

If we are filled with the Holy Spirit, we will worship God. It doesn't matter if we're having a good day or a bad one. Worship is not a sign of happiness—it's a sign of knowing God. Like Paul and Silas, we can praise God no matter where we find ourselves. When we walk with the Spirit, He will help us find joy in God.

▶ What is worship? Read **Psalm 100** and use the following verses to answer the questions.

Verses 1–2	In what ways can we worship God?
Verse 3	Why does He deserve our worship?
Verse 4	In what *other* ways can we worship God?

<table>
<tr><td>Verse
5</td><td>Why else does He deserve our worship?

____

____

______________________________</td></tr>
</table>

▶ Read more about how Israel worshiped God in **Psalm 95:1–5** and **149:1–5**. While we're worshiping God, what attitudes should we have? List at least three.

____

____

▶ Finally, read **Psalm 34:1–3**. Why is David worshiping God? What does he want this worship to do?

____

____

____

7-B The Heart of Worship

Worship is more about the inside than the outside. We can sing the most amazing songs but not believe a word of them. We can do kind things for others—but only for selfish reasons. If worship doesn't come from our heart, what's the point? Why should we magnify God to other people if we're not following Him ourselves?

▶ Read **Isaiah 29:13–14**. God told the prophet that He would show His power to the people of Israel. What was wrong with the way the people worshiped God? (v. 13)

____

____

____

▶ Read **Psalm 69:29–33** and answer the following questions.

◉ As David writes this psalm, is he feeling well and happy? (v. 29) ☐ Yes ☐ No

◉ What does God value more than animal sacrifices? (vv. 30–31)

____

◉ How does this activity help people going through hard times? (vv. 32–33)

____

____

▶ Write **Proverbs 21:3** below.

____

____

____

With sacrifices, the people of Israel showed their sorrow over sin and their gratitude for God's blessing. But a symbol of worship does not matter as much as a heart of worship. A false heart will not glorify God.

▶ So even when no one's around to see us, how can we worship God from our inner being? Read **1 Thessalonians 5:16–18** and list the three things Paul encouraged believers to do.

1. ______________________________________

2. ______________________________________

3. ______________________________________

____

7-C Mary's Worship

Mary was a young woman chosen to fill a marvelous role. She became the mother of Jesus Christ.

▶ Read **Luke 1:26–38** and mark the correct answer to the following questions.

◉ **Verses 26–28 – Who came to visit Mary?**
☐ her future husband, Joseph ☐ the angel Gabriel ☐ David

◉ **Verses 28–30 – The visitor said that Mary had found favor with whom?**
☐ her parents ☐ God ☐ her relative, Elizabeth

◉ **Verse 31 – When Mary gave birth to her son, what name would she give Him?**
☐ Gabriel ☐ David ☐ Jesus

◉ **Verses 32–33 – How long would this child rule from the throne of David?**
☐ three days ☐ thirty-three years ☐ forever

◉ **Verses 34–35 – Since Mary was not married or close to a man, who would miraculously give her a child?**
☐ Joseph ☐ the Holy Spirit ☐ no one

◉ **Verses 36–37 – As a sign that God would keep this promise, who would also have a son?**
☐ the angel ☐ her sister, Judith ☐ her relative, Elizabeth

► Note **verse 38**. Did Mary accept this role?

☐ Yes ☐ No

► While staying with Elizabeth, Mary praised God with a song. Read the song in **Luke 1:46–55** and list two ways that God showed His power or love.

____

____

____

____

____

____

► What attitudes would someone need to sing and believe a song like this?

____

____

Winning Your Race

► Write a short poem or song of worship to God, similar to Psalm 100 or Mary's song in Luke 1. In your text, make sure to explain . . .

⊙ How God has shown you His power or love

⊙ Your attitude toward Him

____

____

____

____

____

____

____

____

____

Vocabulary

- **Repent** – To regret sin and turn back toward God; to ask God to forgive you

- **Sin** – Turning away from God; to break God's Law

- **Deceit** – Lying; making a false statement

- **Bitterness** – Hating someone for past wrongdoing; rehearsing someone's faults in your mind

- **Malice** – The desire to harm someone; hurtful thoughts

- **Confess** – To admit wrongdoing; to reveal what you believe

- **Forgive** – To not hold people's wrongs or failures against them; to give up revenge

8-A The Old and the New

If you've trusted in Jesus Christ, sin is part of your old self. Your flesh wants to do wrong, but the Spirit will challenge you to do right. Will you follow the Spirit or serve your own desires?

▶ In his epistle to the Ephesians, Paul begged Christians to stop committing sins like the evil people around them. What instead should believers do? Read **Ephesians 4:20–24** and fill in the blanks.

⊙ **Verse 22** – We should put off the old _____________________, which is corrupted by desires filled with **deceit**.

⊙ **Verse 23** – We should be renewed in the _______________________________ of our mind.

⊙ **Verse 24** – We should put on the new _____________________, which reflects God's holiness and righteousness.

When we first accept Christ, God begins to transform us to be more like Him. This is God's work, but we can choose to resist Him by going back to our sins.

► Continue reading in **Ephesians 4:25–32**. In your own words, what should we put off and put on?

	Put Off	Put On
Verse 25		
Verses 26–27		
Verse 28		
Verse 29		
Verses 31–32		

► Look again at **Ephesians 4:30**. What do you think it means to "grieve" the Holy Spirit?

____

____

8-B Turning Back to God

► Even when we turn to our old ways and sin, God gives us a path back to Him. Read **1 John 1:5–9** and complete the questions below.

⊙ If God is like a bright light, what is sin like? (vv. 6–7)

____

⊙ If we say that we never sin, what are we doing? (v. 8)

____

⊙ But if we confess our sins, what two things will God do? (v. 9)

____

____

____

The Church in Corinth

Corinth was a very wicked city, and the Corinthian believers were sinning in the same ways as the people around them. So Paul wrote the letter *1 Corinthians* to correct them and show them a better way. In *2 Corinthians*, we find out how the believers responded.

► Read **2 Corinthians 7:8–10** and complete the summaries below.

Verse 8	Paul's first letter made the believers ________________________.
Verse 9	Paul rejoices only because this moved the believers to ________________________.
Verse 10	This is unlike the sorrow of the world, which brings ________________________.

► Based on the verses above, which do you think is most important after you sin?

☐ feeling guilty about sin   ☐ feeling good about yourself   ☐ repenting from sin

John Mark

► In **Acts 13**, we read that the Holy Spirit chose Paul and Barnabas to travel through several cities to preach the gospel. Read the following verses and answer the questions.

⊙ **Verses 4–5** – While Paul and Barnabas shared God's Word, what did John Mark do?

____

⊙ **Verse 13** – What did John do when the group reached the city of Perga?

____

We don't know why John Mark did this, but his decision seemed to break Paul's trust. We can see this at the start of Paul's next missionary journey.

► Read **Acts 15:36–41**. Why did Paul and Barnabas argue and eventually go separate ways?

____

____

► Read **2 Timothy 4:11**, which Paul wrote later in life. How does Paul now describe John Mark?

____

____

Whatever bad decisions John Mark made, he did not give up. He continued to serve God and regained the trust of his friends. Most people now remember him for writing the Gospel of Mark.

▶ Look back at **Ephesians 4:32**. According to Paul, who gave us an example of forgiveness?

____

He is our highest and best example. When we understand how much mercy He has shown us, we'll show mercy to others, as well.

▶ Jesus told His disciples a story to illustrate this kind of forgiveness. Read **Matthew 18:21–35** and fill in the blanks below.

Peter asked Jesus how many times he should forgive someone who wronged him. Peter wondered if _________________ times would be enough. Instead, Jesus said to forgive,
verse 21

even up to _________________________.
verse 22

Jesus told a story about a _________________ who decided to gather all the debts
verse 23

owed to him. There was a servant who owed him 10,000 _____________________________.
verse 24

Since the man was not able to pay, the king ordered that the man be sold along with

everything he had, including his wife and _________________________.
verse 25

The servant begged for patience, saying that he would pay back _________________________.
verse 26

So the king had mercy and _________________________ the debt for him.
verse 27

But then the man found a fellow _________________________ who owed him just 100
verse 28

_________________________. While strangling the man, he demanded to be repaid.
verse 28

The man who owed money begged for patience, but the servant refused and threw him into

_________________________.
verse 30

When the king found out what had happened, he summoned the unforgiving man and

called him a _________________________. The king asked why he had not shown the
verse 32

same _________________________ that the king had shown. So the king angrily sent the
verse 33

man to the _________________________ until the old debt was paid.
verse 34

▶ Look again at **Matthew 18:35**. How would you summarize the lesson of this story?

____

____

____

____

Winning Your Race

▶ Describe a possible negative consequence for each of the following sins:

⊙ Lying – ____

____

____

⊙ Saying cruel things about a friend – _______________________________

____

____

⊙ Valuing anything more than your relationship to God – _______________

____

____

▶ It's easy to say "sorry" after someone catches us doing wrong. But think about the last time you told God that you were sorry for your sin *before* anyone noticed something bad.

⊙ Do you have anything to confess to God? If so, take a moment to do so now.

⊙ Do you have something to confess to someone else? If so, commit yourself to apologizing and making things right as soon as you can.

▶ Can you think of an offense you have trouble forgiving? Without putting yourself in an unsafe situation, how can you better show mercy?

____

____

____

____

Path of the Righteous

Vocabulary

- **Meditate** – To think deeply and continually about something

- **Chaff** – The empty husks left behind after threshing grain; the useless part of the plant

9-A The Two Ways

To run our race well, we must stay on the right track. There's no point running hard and fast if we're running in the wrong direction. Thankfully, Scripture describes our two choices—God's way and the way of sin.

► Read **Psalm 1** and complete the following summaries.

Verse 1	Blessed is the person who . . . • Does not walk with the ____________________ • Does not stand in the way with ____________________ • Does not sit with ____________________
Verse 2	The blessed person takes delight in God's Law and ____________________ on it day and night.
Verse 3	This person is like a fruitful, enduring ______________ planted by a river.
Verse 4	But the ____________________ are like **chaff** blown away by the wind.
Verses 5-6	The ____________________ will not stand in the judgment, and their path will end in disaster. But God knows the way of the ____________________.

- ⊙ Why do you think the writer compares a righteous person to a tree?

  ____

  ____

  ____

- ⊙ Why do you think the writer compares ungodly or wicked people to chaff?

  ____

  ____

▶ Jesus talked about two ways, as well. Read **Matthew 7:13–14** and then answer the questions for each gate.

	The Narrow Gate	The Wide Gate
Where does it lead?		
How many people take it?		

9-B The Fall of Lot

Abraham (first called Abram) was the father of the nation of Israel, but not all of his relatives followed God. His nephew Lot made some bad decisions that put him in the path of God's judgment.

▶ Read **Genesis 13:8–13** and answer the following questions.

- ⊙ When Abram and Lot needed to divide their flocks and go separate ways, where did Lot choose to go? (vv. 11–12)

  ____

- ⊙ How are the people of Sodom described? (v. 13)

  ____

- ⊙ What was the Lord going to do to the two cities near Lot? (v. 10)

  ____

These verses do not say that Lot turned from God in this moment. But as Lot lived closer and closer to sinful people, he began to suffer consequences from their wickedness.

▶ In **Genesis 14:11–16**, Lot got caught up in a war between Sodom and other nations.

- ⊙ What did Abram have to do for Lot? (vv. 14–16)

  ____

- ⊙ Where was Lot now living? (v. 12) _______________________________________

In Genesis 18, God told Abraham that He would soon destroy the cities of Sodom and Gomorrah. The sins of the people were so great that God would not delay His judgment. Abraham knew that Lot was living in Sodom, so he pleaded for mercy. The Lord agreed that if there were at least ten righteous people living in Sodom, He would spare it.

▶ Unfortunately, there were not even ten people in Sodom who followed God. But God loved Abraham enough to spare his nephew Lot. Read the following verses from **Genesis 19** and mark the correct ending to each sentence.

Verses 1–3: God sent two angels into the city, and Lot begged them to . . .

- ☐ go away and never return.
- ☐ rest in his house overnight.
- ☐ destroy the city—except for his family, friends, and the merchants he traded with.

Verses 4–8: The men of Sodom wanted to harm the two angels, so Lot . . .

- ☐ gathered his weapons and prepared to fight.
- ☐ offered the men his daughters, instead.
- ☐ threw the angels out of his house.

Verses 9–11: Before the mob could overrun the house, the angels . . .

- ☐ struck the men blind.
- ☐ fled out of the city.
- ☐ threw Lot out the door.

Verses 12–13: The angels told Lot to leave with his family because . . .

- ☐ his daughters would find terrible husbands here.
- ☐ the mob was too strong for the angels.
- ☐ the angels were about to destroy the entire city.

Verses 14–17: In the morning, Lot, his wife, and his daughters . . .

- ☐ had to be dragged out of the city by the angels.
- ☐ stayed in the city.
- ☐ left the city quickly.

Verses 23–28: When God destroyed the valley with fire and burning rock . . .

- ☐ Lot and his family followed the instructions from the angels.
- ☐ Lot's wife looked back and became a pillar of salt.
- ☐ Lot's daughters looked back and became pillars of salt.

We read in 2 Peter 2:6–8 that Lot was righteous. However, by walking in the ways of wicked people, Lot put his entire family in danger. Lot himself survived, but he lost much of what he loved. He spent his last days living in a cave.

Some people fall away from God little by little, diving deeper and deeper into sin until they become overwhelmed by the consequences. It's so easy to take small steps away from God's path.

But there are sign posts to keep us on the right track. We have Scripture, the Spirit, and other mature believers to remind us what's true and good. Every day and every moment, we must choose to follow God.

▶ Read the following passages and match them to their main ideas.

A. Psalm 119:9–11	B. Proverbs 3:5–6	C. Matthew 7:21	D. Philippians 2:12–13	E. Hebrews 12:1–3

	Trust God instead of your own understanding. Follow God in all your ways, and He will direct your path.
	Throw off sin and everything that hinders you. Run the race with perseverance, focusing on Jesus.
	If Christ has saved you, you should "work out" this salvation to show respect for God's work in you.
	You can keep your way pure by following God's Word. To avoid sin, you should hide God's Word in your heart.
	Not everyone who calls Jesus "Lord" will enter His kingdom. To enter, they must do the will of the Father.

▶ Given what you read in the passages above, mark the following sentences as true or false.

We should listen to wise advice, but the greatest wisdom is in Scripture.	☐ True	☐ False
Little sins are OK as long as we keep them from becoming big sins.	☐ True	☐ False
People follow Jesus by saying that they follow Jesus.	☐ True	☐ False
By memorizing Scripture, we can remind ourselves to do right.	☐ True	☐ False
We do good things so we can force God to allow us into heaven.	☐ True	☐ False

▶ Choose one of the false statements above and rewrite it correctly.

____

____

____

Winning Your Race

▶ When following God's way, it's important to get good advice from wise people. The following is a list of different sources of advice. Rank each source from the most important (**1**) to the least important (**14**). In the blank rows, include two sources that are unique to your life.

	A. Artists and musicians		**H.** My parents or guardians	
	B. Athletes and sports figures		**I.** My siblings	
	C. Fictional characters		**J.** Pastors or church leaders	
	D. God's Word		**K.** People who make hilarious videos	
	E. Government officials		**L.** Scientists and medical doctors	
	F. Mature Christians who know me		**M.**	
	G. My friends		**N.**	

▶ For each question below, write the **letters** of the sources that could give you the right advice.

◉ How far is the planet Jupiter from Earth? _______________________________________

◉ How can I get better at my favorite hobby? _______________________________________

◉ My friend is having a difficult time. How can I help? _______________________________

◉ How can I stay safe during dangerous weather? ___________________________________

◉ How can I grow closer to God? ____

▶ Take a moment to think about your choice of friends, activities, and entertainment. Are there some that influence you toward evil? Ask God to help you identify bad influences and replace them with good, wise ones.

Honor and Obedience

Vocabulary

- **Honor** – To show great respect or reverence; to value the good in someone

- **Commandment** – A law or rule; in Exodus, the Ten Commandments begin God's Law

- **Obey** – To do what someone else says to do; to comply or submit your will to another

- **Ark of the Covenant** – A gold-plated chest containing important items from Israel's history, including the Ten Commandments; a symbol of God's presence with His people

10-A The Command to Honor

When God brought Israel out of Egypt, the people had spent hundreds of years in a wicked country. They did not know much about God or what He expected from them. So God began to teach the Israelites through His Law.

The most important part of the Law is the **Ten Commandments**. Christians should still follow these commands today. They show us how to reflect God's character.

▶ Review these commands in **Exodus 20:1–17** and answer the questions below.

⊙ The first four commands are about our relationship with God. Who are the other six commands about? (vv. 12–17)

____

⊙ What is the fifth command? (v. 12)

____

⊙ What promise did God give along with this command? (v. 12)

____

____

God had promised the Israelites a land to call home. To enjoy this blessing, the people needed to obey God's commands. They could follow God to see Him fulfill His promises.

▶ We honor when we show respect and value the good in someone. Complete the following:

⊙ Describe one good thing that a parent or guardian gives you every day.

____

⊙ Describe one good thing that a parent or guardian has taught you.

____

____

⊙ Are your parents or guardians absolutely perfect, with zero flaws? ☐ Yes ☐ No

⊙ So when you think about the good they show you, what are you most thankful for?

____

____

▶ In the New Testament, the Apostle Paul notes one very important way for children to show honor in their families. Read **Ephesians 6:1–3** and write the commands given in these verses.

⊙ **Verse 1** – ____

⊙ **Verse 2** – ____

All children should honor their parents however they can. When we're young and living at home, honor looks like obedience. Our parents and guardians teach us to obey so that when we're adults, we can make wise decisions on our own. By obeying when we're young, we learn to follow God and do right when we're older.

We do not obey just for the sake of obeying. We obey to show love and honor to others.

10-B Samuel's Obedience

Eli was an Israelite priest at the Tabernacle in a town called Shiloh. His two sons, Hophni and Phinehas, also worked with him. The three men lived in the era of judges, before Israel had any kings or queens.

▶ Read **1 Samuel 2:12–17** and answer the following questions.

⊙ How are Eli's sons described? (v. 12)

____

⊙ It was the job of priests to help the people make offerings to God. But what were Eli's sons doing? (vv. 15–17)

____

____

Eli's sons committed many other terrible sins in Shiloh, and they did it all while pretending to serve the Lord. They were not acting like priests of God at all. They were selfish and mistreated people to suit their own desires.

▶ Continue reading in **1 Samuel 2:22–25** and answer the following.

⊙ After hearing about his sons' behavior, what did Eli do? (vv. 23–25)

____

⊙ Did this help? Did the sons change their ways? (v. 25)　　☐ Yes　☐ No

Eli had an easier time with a boy named Samuel. When Samuel was born, his mother dedicated him to be a priest for God. So Eli raised Samuel in Shiloh, teaching him how to serve in the Tabernacle.

▶ But one night, God gave Samuel a difficult task. Read **1 Samuel 3:1–18** and order the events below from **1** to **7**.

	Samuel ran to Eli and said, "Here I am." Eli said he had not called Samuel. This happened three times.
	After going back to bed, Samuel did and said exactly what Eli told him to.
	The third time Samuel went to Eli, the priest realized that God was calling Samuel.
	After being asked, Samuel gave God's message to Eli. The old priest said that God would do what He thought was good.
	God told Samuel that He would judge Eli and his sons for allowing their sin to continue.
	Eli told Samuel that the next time he heard the voice, he should reply, "Speak, Lord," and say that he was listening.
	Samuel was lying down for the night, when suddenly the Lord called to him.

As Samuel grew up, he continued to follow God. More and more people recognized Samuel as a prophet of the Lord, and God blessed his ministry.

But what happened to Hophni and Phinehas? When Israel went to war with the Philistine nation, Hophni and Phinehas brought the **Ark of the Covenant** as a sort of good-luck charm.

▶ Read **1 Samuel 4:10–11**. Did Israel's plan work?　　☐ Yes　☐ No

▶ Read **1 Samuel 4:14–18**. What happened when Eli heard the news?

____

____

10-C Learning Submission

We submit when we serve others and put their needs above our own. We can submit by obeying, but we can also submit without being told to do anything. Submission should come from a love for others, and it's a necessary ingredient for almost every relationship.

▶ How can we serve the people around us? Read the passages below and complete the summaries.

Ephesians 5:18–21	Believers should be filled with the Spirit, praising God together, giving thanks to Him in all things, and _______________________ to each other out of respect for Him.
Ephesians 5:22	_______________ should submit to their own husbands as to the Lord.
Ephesians 5:25	_______________ should love their wives like Christ loves the Church.
Ephesians 6:1	Children should obey their _______________ in the Lord.
Ephesians 6:5–8	_______________ should obey their _______________. They should work with sincerity, doing good for the Lord's sake.
Ephesians 6:9	And masters should _______________ _______________, without threatening them. We all have one Master in heaven who treats us equally.
James 4:7	Believers should submit to _______________ and resist the devil.
1 Peter 2:13	Believers should submit to every _______________ _______________ for the Lord's sake.

Our relationships can look much different than the ones in the early days of the New Testament. In the Roman Empire of that time, there were many slave-owners, cruel government officials, and husbands who treated their wives like property. But Paul, James, and Peter encouraged believers to love and serve regardless of the culture around them.

No matter the situation, we can share God's love. People may fail us or mistreat us, but we can submit out of a respect for God. By serving others, we can show them how God has helped us.

Winning Your Race

▶ Take some time to evaluate how well you show honor at home. For each statement, rate how often it is true for you, from **1** to **5**.

	Rarely		Sometimes		Usually
When a parent or guardian tells me to do something, I do it as soon as I can.	1	2	3	4	5
I thank my parents or guardians for everything they do for me.	1	2	3	4	5
When I make a mistake at home, I take responsibility for it instead of blaming others.	1	2	3	4	5
I pay attention to the things that my parents or guardians tell me. I actively listen to them.	1	2	3	4	5
When I disagree with my parents or guardians, I talk with them calmly and respectfully.	1	2	3	4	5
When I do not understand them, I try to see things from their point of view.	1	2	3	4	5
When they make a decision I don't like, I submit anyway and do not complain.	1	2	3	4	5

To Help or Rebel

Vocabulary

- **Rebel** – To oppose a ruler or some other authority, often with hatred or violence
- **Firstborn** – The first child of a husband and wife
- **Justice** – The state of being just, lawful, or right; fair punishment for wrongdoing
- **Vow** – A serious, unbreakable promise, sometimes to God Himself

11-A David and Absalom

David's **firstborn** son was named Amnon. Even though Amnon was in line to become king after his father, he was a very wicked man. One day, he hurt his half-sister Tamar deeply. Under the Old Testament Law, Amnon should have been punished severely and maybe even executed. King David was very angry with his son but did nothing.

David's third son Absalom took the crime much more seriously. But instead of seeking **justice** for what Amnon did, Absalom chose to take revenge.

▶ Read **2 Samuel 13:22–29** and answer the following questions.

- How long did Absalom wait before doing anything? (v. 23) _______________________

- When it was time to shear his flocks of sheep, Absalom threw a party for his brothers. What did he beg King David to do? (vv. 26–27)

  ____

- What did Absalom tell his servants to do? (vv. 28–29)

  ____

  ____

David mourned for his firstborn, and Absalom fled to another country. The father and son did not see each other for a long time.

After three years, David's top general, a man named Joab, saw that the king was still upset over Absalom. So Joab convinced David to bring Absalom back to Israel. Absalom could live in his own house, but he could not see the king. Eventually, after two more years, David and Absalom finally met again and embraced.

▶ Meanwhile, Absalom began to capture the attention of the people. How does **2 Samuel 14:25–26** describe him?

____

____

▶ Read **2 Samuel 15:1–6** and complete the summaries below.

Verse 1	Absalom gathered a chariot, some ___________________, and _____________ men to run ahead of him.
Verse 2	Absalom rose early each morning to stand by the way near the _____________ of the city. He greeted everyone coming to see the king for judgment.
Verse 3	Absalom told these people that their cause was _________________________ _____________________, but also that the king had no one to see them about it.
Verse 4	Absalom then wished out loud that he were _____________ of the land so that he could give people justice.
Verses 5–6	Absalom continued greeting the people. In this way, he _____________ the hearts of the Israelites.

Instead of helping his father, Absalom built up his own reputation and popularity. Absalom saw David's failures as a chance to seize the kingdom for himself.

▶ Continue reading in **2 Samuel 15:7–14** and mark the following statements as true or false.

Absalom told David that he needed to go to Hebron and fulfill a **vow** to worship the Lord.	☐ True	☐ False
Absalom secretly planned a celebration for his father.	☐ True	☐ False
All the men following Absalom to Hebron knew what he planned to do.	☐ True	☐ False
While Absalom stayed in Hebron, his followers kept decreasing.	☐ True	☐ False
After David heard from the messenger, he thought that most of Israel had decided to make Absalom king.	☐ True	☐ False
David chose to stay in Jerusalem and fight against his son.	☐ True	☐ False

11-B Absalom's Fate

Absalom's plot to overthrow David seemed to be going well. Many people admired Absalom and supported his rebellion. Soon, Absalom marched with his soldiers into the capital city of Jerusalem.

But Absalom was not content just to be king. He wanted to humiliate his father. As the new ruler of Jerusalem, Absalom moved into David's house and hurt the people there— just to show them that he was in control. Absalom became even worse than his brother Amnon had been.

► Eventually, Absalom decided to gather an army and hunt down his father. He wanted to kill David and every man who helped the king. Read **2 Samuel 18:1–17** and match each sentence below to its best ending.

Verses 1–4 – David divided his army into three groups, but he . . .	**A.** got his head stuck in an oak tree.
Verse 5 – When David told his commanders not to harm Absalom, all the king's people . . .	**B.** heard what he said.
Verses 6–8 – After the battle, 20,000 people were dead, and David's soldiers had . . .	**C.** did not go to the battle.
Verse 9 – While riding on his mule, Absalom . . .	**D.** killed Absalom and buried him in a pit.
Verses 10–12 – One of David's soldiers saw Absalom and . . .	**E.** told Joab what he found.
Verses 14–17 – Joab and some of his men found the tree and . . .	**F.** defeated the rest of Israel's forces.

► Read **2 Samuel 18:32–33**. How did David react to the news about Absalom?

____

____

► Imagine you are Absalom before he killed Amnon or started the rebellion. How could you seek justice and still honor your father the king?

____

____

____

____

____

11-C Saul and Jonathan

Before David, Saul was the king over Israel. He ruled during a time of great conflict, when the Philistines were Israel's greatest enemy. Saul led the Israelites into battle, and he was supported by his son Jonathan.

▶ Read the following verses from **1 Samuel 14** and mark the correct ending to each sentence.

Verses 11–15: Jonathan and his armor-bearer started the battle by . . .

| ☐ attacking the Philistines all by themselves. | ☐ taking control of Israel's army from Saul. | ☐ running away from the Philistine camp. |

Verses 23–24: Saul wanted to kill the Philistines so badly that he . . .

| ☐ prayed to God for help. | ☐ cursed anyone who would eat before the enemy was dead. | ☐ made sure his army got plenty of food and rest. |

Verses 25–27: Jonathan ate some honey from the forest because he . . .

| ☐ didn't care about disobeying his father. | ☐ had an irresistible love for sweet things. | ☐ had not heard about his father's curse. |

Verses 28–30: Jonathan thought that his father should have . . .

| ☐ allowed Jonathan to lead the army. | ☐ let the army eat so they could fight better. | ☐ given some of the honey to the priests. |

Verses 31–33: After the battle, the Israelites were so hungry that they . . .

| ☐ couldn't fight for weeks. | ☐ ate some of the Philistines' animals raw. | ☐ died. |

Verses 37–39: When Saul heard no answer from God, he tried to find out . . .

| ☐ if he had built his altar incorrectly. | ☐ if one of his men had stolen something. | ☐ who in Israel's army had committed sin. |

Verses 43–44: When Saul found out that Jonathan had eaten honey, he said . . .

| ☐ that Jonathan must die. | ☐ that he was sorry. | ☐ that everything was fine. |

Verses 45–46: Then the people around Saul . . .

| ☐ prevented him from killing Jonathan. | ☐ helped him execute Jonathan. | ☐ attacked the king and killed him. |

After the young David became a hero to Israel, Saul drove himself mad with hatred and jealousy. But Jonathan loved David and became a good friend to him. Saul wanted David dead, but Jonathan protected David while supporting the king however he could.

► Jonathan continued fighting alongside his father for the good of Israel. Read **1 Samuel 31:1–2**. Where did Jonathan die?

____

Saul should have been a much better father and king. But Saul's sin did not keep Jonathan from being a great son, friend, and leader.

Winning Your Race

► What is one way that God continues supporting you even after you sin?

____

____

____

► What should you do after sinning against someone in your family?

____

____

____

____

► Think back to the last time a person in authority failed you in some way. How could you have responded better?

____

____

____

____

Vocabulary

- **The Heart** – Used in Scripture to mean our deepest beliefs and attitudes; our core, inner self

- **Pharisees** – A Jewish religious group that added their own rules to God's law

- **Tradition** – A custom that is practiced over a long time; a long-held set of beliefs

- **Hypocrite** – Someone who pretends to be better than they are; a person who contradicts their words with their actions

- **Defile** – To corrupt; to make unholy or impure

- **Persecute** – To continually oppress or mistreat people, often for their religion or ethnicity

- **Abomination** – Something that is hated, disgusting, or detestable

12-A The Nature of Our Hearts

▶ Read **Matthew 15:1–20** and answer the questions below.

⊙ What did the **Pharisees** accuse Jesus' disciples of doing? (v. 2)

____

⊙ When possible, is it a good idea to wash your hands before eating?　☐ Yes　☐ No

⊙ If we don't have the chance to wash our hands, do we sin against God?　☐ Yes　☐ No

⊙ What did Jesus say that the Pharisees were doing?

Verse 3: _______________________________________

____

Verses 7–8: _____________________________________

____

⊙ What did Jesus call the Pharisees and scribes? (v. 7) _____________________

◉ Instead of helping people understand God's Word and follow Him, the Pharisees were making up their own rules. According to Jesus, what were they like? (v. 14)

____

◉ Jesus explained to His disciples that we do not **defile** ourselves by what we eat. Instead, where do sin and evil come from? (vv. 16–20)

____

▶ Everything we say or do comes from the heart. Read the following passages and complete the summaries.

Genesis 6:5	God saw that the thoughts of human hearts remained ________________.
Deuteronomy 4:29	Moses told the people of Israel that if they sought the Lord with all their heart and soul, they would ________________ Him.
2 Chronicles 12:13–14	King Rehoboam did evil because he did not ________________ the Lord with his heart.
Proverbs 4:23	We should keep guard over our ________________ because our life flows from it.
Matthew 12:33–34	Our mouth ________________ whatever overflows from our hearts.

12-B Loving God Wholeheartedly

Our hearts will lean toward good or evil depending on what we value. If we want what God wants, we will naturally follow Him. If we submit to sinful desires, we will always do wrong.

▶ Where should we focus our hearts? Read **Matthew 6:19–24** and answer the following.

◉ What happens to earthly treasures? (v. 19)

____

____

◉ What will last longer than earthly treasures? (v. 20)

____

◉ Why can't we serve two "masters" equally? (v. 24)

____

____

► A wealthy young man once came to talk with Jesus. Read **Matthew 19:16–26** and mark the best ending to each sentence.

Verse 16: The man asked Jesus what he could do to . . .

| ☐ have eternal life. | ☐ get even richer. | ☐ become wiser. |

Verses 17–19: Jesus told the man to . . .

| ☐ wash himself every day. | ☐ keep God's commands. | ☐ pray in the Temple. |

Verse 19: Jesus summarized these rules with the command to . . .

| ☐ love your neighbor as yourself. | ☐ avoid doing anything that seems bad. | ☐ perform all the rituals in the Law of Moses. |

Verse 21: The man asked what else he was lacking, so Jesus told him to . . .

| ☐ study at the Temple in Jerusalem. | ☐ be willing to suffer more for God. | ☐ sell what he owned and give to the poor. |

Verse 22: When the man heard this, he . . .

| ☐ got angry and began to argue with Jesus. | ☐ immediately did what Jesus said. | ☐ left in sorrow because he had many things. |

► Look again at **Matthew 19:23–25**. In your own words, why can it be difficult for a wealthy person to enter God's kingdom?

____

____

____

► Finally, read about another wealthy man—Zacchaeus the tax collector. Read **Luke 19:1–10** and answer the following questions.

⊙ What did Zacchaeus do in order to see Jesus? (vv. 3–4)

____

⊙ How did Zacchaeus respond to Jesus? (v. 6)

____

⊙ How did Zacchaeus show his repentance from sin? (v. 8)

____

____

12-C Revealing Our Hearts

▶ If we love God wholeheartedly, we will put that love into action. Read **Romans 12:9–21**. After thinking about this passage, mark each statement below as true or false.

If we have love, we will honor others above ourselves.	☐ True	☐ False
We can love others, but we shouldn't love those who **persecute** us.	☐ True	☐ False
It's our duty to repay every evil thing done to us.	☐ True	☐ False
We can love and support people whether they're happy or sad.	☐ True	☐ False
Love means giving to those in need, even if they are enemies.	☐ True	☐ False
Real love will give us humility. We will want to befriend all kinds of people, not just the popular or rich.	☐ True	☐ False
If we don't punish people who hurt us, no one will.	☐ True	☐ False

▶ In **Proverbs 6:16–19**, you'll find a list of seven **abominations** to God. Write this list below, and then draw an imaginary person who pictures all seven of these things. Where you can, draw arrows from the list to the parts of your picture.

1. _______________________________

2. _______________________________

3. _______________________________

   ____

4. _______________________________

   ____

   ____

5. _______________________________

   ____

6. _______________________________

   ____

7. _______________________________

   ____

Winning Your Race

Christians must be good from the inside out. If our heart doesn't follow God, it will be difficult or impossible to show the kind of love in Romans 12.

► Look again at the list in **Proverbs 6:16–19**. How would each behavior or attitude change if someone had a heart that loved God? In other words, what is the opposite of each abomination?

1. ____

____

2. ____

____

3. ____

____

4. ____

____

5. ____

____

6. ____

____

7. ____

____

63

Vocabulary

- **_Forerunner_** – Someone who goes ahead of another, often to prepare the way

- **_Baptize_** – To use water to symbolize someone's new relationship with God

13-A John's Birth

Before Jesus began His ministry on Earth, God chose a **_forerunner_** to tell people that the Messiah would come soon. This forerunner was named John. He dedicated his life to preparing the way for Jesus.

▶ If it weren't for God, John's life could not even have begun. Read **Luke 1:5–12** and answer the following questions.

⊙ The writer Luke introduces John's parents in **verse 5**. What were their names?

____

⊙ How does the writer describe these two people? (v. 6)

____

____

⊙ Could they have children together? (v. 7) ☐ Yes ☐ No

Why or why not? _______________________________

____

____

⊙ What was Zechariah (Zacharias) doing when he saw the angel? (vv. 8–11)

____

____

► Continue reading **Luke 1:13–17** and fill in the blanks to summarize the message that God sent through the angel Gabriel.

Verse 13	Zechariah and Elizabeth would have a son to be named ________________.
Verses 14–15	Many would rejoice over this child because he would be great in the Lord's sight. He would not drink wine nor ________________.
Verse 15	He would be filled with the ________________ even in Elizabeth's womb.
Verse 16	He would turn many in Israel back to the ________________.
Verse 17	He would serve with the same spirit and power as ________________, and he would prepare the Jewish people for the Lord.

► Read **Luke 1:18–23**. Since Zechariah did not believe God's message at first, how did the angel prove God's power?

____

► Finally, read **Luke 1:57–66** and answer the following:

- ⊙ Did God fulfill His promises? ☐ Yes ☐ No
- ⊙ Did Elizabeth and Zechariah name their son John? ☐ Yes ☐ No
- ⊙ What did Zechariah do the moment he could speak again?

____

13-B John's Ministry

Shortly after John's birth, Zechariah praised God for remembering His promises to Israel. The Messiah would bring salvation, and John had a part in this plan.

► Read part of Zechariah's psalm in **Luke 1:76–79**. In your own words, how would John one day help the people of Israel?

____

____

____

► Read **Luke 1:80**. Where did John prepare before beginning his ministry?

____

► When John grew up and began to serve, his ministry seemed very unusual. Read how he fulfilled God's promises in **Matthew 3:1–12**. Then use the verses to complete the crossword puzzle.

- **Verse 1** – John came ___ in the wilderness of Judea.
- **Verse 2** – John told people to ___ because the kingdom of heaven was near.
- **Verse 3** – The prophet ___ foretold John's message and ministry.
- **Verse 4** – John wore clothes made from camel's hair, and he ate locusts and wild ___.
- **Verse 6** – People were ___ by John as they confessed their sins.
- **Verse 7** – When some religious leaders came to see John, he called them a group of ___.
- **Verse 10** – John warned that every ___ with no good fruit would be cut down and burned.
- **Verse 11** – John said that the One coming after him would baptize with the ___ ___ and fire.

13-C The True Vine

We don't read in Scripture that John was especially smart, strong, or good-looking. No, he was great because God was *with him greatly*. The Spirit worked through him just as the Spirit can work through us today. We might not wear camel skin or baptize people in the Jordan River, but we can still dedicate ourselves to Jesus.

► The religious leaders in John's day were like trees with no good fruit. They had no dedication or love for God. Read what Jesus said in **Luke 6:43–45**.

- Can a bad tree produce truly good fruit?   ☐ Yes   ☐ No

- What comes out of a good person's heart? ____

- What comes out of an evil person's heart? ____

We must be good from the inside out. But how?

► Read what Jesus taught His disciples in **John 15:1–6** and fill in the blanks below.

Jesus is the true ________________. The Father takes away every ____________________ that does not bear ________________. For the branches that *are* fruitful, the Father ____________________________ them so that they will produce even more.

We believers should ____________________ in Jesus just like He lives in us. We cannot bear fruit without Him. The branches who don't stay connected with Him will wither and be thrown into the ______________.

► Continue reading in **John 15:7–12** and answer the following.

◉ What happens when we bear good fruit and reveal ourselves to be Jesus' disciples? (v. 8)

____

◉ Who is our example of obedience, joy, and love? (vv. 9–12) __________________________

Winning Your Race

► Look again at the promise in **John 15:7.** What must be true for us to receive this promise?

____

____

► What do you think it means for Jesus' words to be in us?

____

____

____

____

____

► How will His words affect what you ask Him for?

____

____

____

____

____

Courage to Stand

Vocabulary

- **Testimony** – A record or witness, often of something important

- **Beelzebub / Beelzebul** – A name used in Scripture to refer to Satan or another demon

14-A John Baptizes Jesus

John the Baptist had spent his entire ministry preparing people for the coming Messiah. One day, Jesus finally came from Galilee to see him.

▶ Read **Matthew 3:11–17** and answer the following.

⊙ When Jesus arrived, what did He want John to do? (v. 13)

____

⊙ At first, how did John feel about this? (vv. 11, 14)

____

____

⊙ Why did Jesus want to be baptized? (v. 15)

____

⊙ What happened after Jesus came out of the Jordan River?

Verse 16 – The sky opened up, and the _______________________________ descended

like a _________________ to rest on Jesus.

Verse 17 – A voice from heaven said "_______________________________________

____

____ "

This event marked the beginning of Jesus' earthly ministry. John's mission as forerunner had been fulfilled. The Messiah had arrived.

But John still needed courage. He had made some enemies during his ministry, and one of those was King Herod. The king had broken the Law by taking his brother's wife for his own. John condemned the king's wrongdoing, just like many prophets had throughout Israel's history. Herod's new wife was so angry that Herod threw John into prison.

This would greatly discourage most people. John believed that the Messiah would save Israel and take away the sins of the world. How was that possible if John, the Messiah's forerunner, was a prisoner? John probably wondered about God's plan.

▶ Read **Matthew 11:1–6** and fill in the blanks to complete the summaries.

Verses 2–3	John sent his disciples to ask Jesus if He was ________________________ ________________________ or if they should look for another.
Verses 4–5	Jesus said to tell John what they would ____________ and ____________. People were being healed while hearing the good news of Christ.
Verse 6	____________ is the person who does not take offense at Jesus.

▶ Continue reading in **Matthew 11:7–11**. What did Jesus think of John?

____

____

14-B John's Death

▶ Read **Mark 6:17–29** and match each statement to the correct ending.

	Herod's wife Herodias wanted John to be . . .	**A.** promised to give her almost anything she wanted.
	But Herod feared John as a holy man, so he . . .	**B.** executed John by beheading.
	On Herod's birthday, the daughter of Herodias . . .	**C.** listened to him and kept him safe in prison.
	Herod was so pleased with her that he . . .	**D.** asked for the head of John the Baptist.
	After talking to Herodias, the daughter . . .	**E.** danced for Herod and his party guests.
	Herod regretted his promise, but he . . .	**F.** buried his body.
	When John's disciples heard, they . . .	**G.** put to death.

Herod was a wicked king who let others push him into more wickedness. His sinful decisions continued to haunt him.

► Read **Mark 6:7–16**. When Herod heard about Jesus' ministry, what did he think had happened?

____

____

On one hand, these verses reveal Herod's fear and guilt. On the other hand, they show how powerfully God worked through John. His ministry reflected Jesus so much that people thought the two were the same person.

► While in prison before his death, John continued preaching and talking to the king. Where do you think John found the courage to do this?

____

____

____

14-C Standing for Jesus

► In **John 5**, Jesus listed some **testimonies** of His authority. Jesus is equal to God the Father, and indeed God Himself. Read the verses below and write *who* or *what* pointed to Jesus' power.

⊙ **Verses 33–35:** ____

⊙ **Verse 36:** ____

⊙ **Verses 37–38:** ____

⊙ **Verses 46–47:** ____

John the Baptist was the last person in a long plan to reveal the Messiah. And now that Jesus has lived, taught, died, and risen again, believers today can point people to Him. We can be living, breathing, outspoken testimonies to His love and truth.

► But there's a cost to following Jesus openly. Read what He taught in **Matthew 10:24-42** and mark the correct ending to each sentence.

Verses 24–25: If people called Jesus a demon or false god, then they would . . .		
☐ call His followers worse.	☐ treat His followers better.	☐ eventually repent.

Verses 26–28: We shouldn't fear those who persecute or kill us, but rather . . .		
☐ the One who can judge our body and soul.	☐ the evil masterminds behind them.	☐ our closest friends.

- [ ] little children.
- [ ] our political leaders.
- [ ] sparrows.

- [ ] we will not be persecuted.
- [ ] He will do the same for us before the Father.
- [ ] Jesus will destroy those who mistreat us.

- [ ] success, wealth, and an easy life.
- [ ] conflict between family members.
- [ ] constant feelings of happiness and peace.

- [ ] face God's wrath.
- [ ] never sin.
- [ ] receive a reward.

Winning Your Race

▶ God's approval matters more than the approval of anyone else. Describe something good that's difficult to do because other people might think badly of you.

____

____

____

____

Vocabulary

- **Foolishness** – Refusing to learn; using knowledge poorly; the opposite of wisdom

- **Proverb** – A wise saying; a short statement that teaches a general principle

15-A Fools Hate Wisdom

▶ Read the following **proverbs** and note the differences between those who are wise and those who are foolish. Complete the summaries.

	The wise will . . .	The foolish will . . .
Proverbs 1:7	_______________ the Lord	_______________ wisdom and instruction
Proverbs 10:19	Often refrain from speaking	_______________ _______________
Proverbs 12:16	_______________ _______________	Show their frustration immediately
Proverbs 12:18	Speak to bring _______________	Speak words that stab like a _______________
Proverbs 14:8	_______________ their ways	Deceive themselves and others
Proverbs 14:9	Be kind and accepting	Mock at _______________ _______________

	The wise will . . .	The foolish will . . .
Proverbs 14:16	Cautiously turn from _____________	________________________ ________________________ ________________________
Proverbs 15:5	Listen to those who correct them	________________________ ________________________
Proverbs 29:8	Turn away _____________________	________________________ ________________________

▶ Based on these verses, how would you describe a wise person?

____

____

▶ How would you describe a foolish person?

____

____

15-B Ahab and Jezebel

In the Old Testament, many of Israel's leaders rejected God. Two of the most evil and foolish were a king and queen who ruled in the time of the prophet Elijah.

▶ Read **1 Kings 16:29–33** and answer the following questions.

◉ Who was the son of Omri? (v. 29) _____________________

◉ How long was he king of Israel? (v. 29) _____________________________

◉ What made him special in Israel's history? (v. 30)

____

____

◉ What especially wicked things did he do? (v. 31)

   1. He married _______________________________, the daughter of a Sidonian king.

   2. He served and worshiped _______________________.

When God gave the Israelites His Law, He told them not to marry people who worshiped false gods. By marrying Jezebel, Ahab disobeyed God and set a bad example for the people of Israel.

▶ Look back at **Judges 3:5–6**, when the Israelites first came to the land of Canaan. What happened when the Israelites married people who served false gods?

____

▶ Elijah the prophet confronted Ahab. Read **1 Kings 17:1**. What happened because of Israel's sin?

____

God took care of those who followed Him, including Elijah. But the kingdom of Israel faced great hardships, and many people suffered.

▶ What should Ahab and Jezebel have done at this point?

____

____

▶ Read **1 Kings 18:4**. Why did Obadiah, the master of Ahab's house, try to hide God's prophets?

____

▶ Eventually, Elijah decided to meet with Ahab. Read **1 Kings 18:17–19**.

   ◉ What did Ahab call Elijah? (v. 17) _______________________________________

   ◉ But what was Israel's real problem? (v. 18)

   ____

   ____

   ◉ What did Elijah challenge Ahab to do? (v. 19)

   ____

   ____

15-C Testing Ba'al

Israel suffered because the people and their leaders would not stop worshiping false gods. Different cities might have their own favorite *Ba'al* for their own favorite religion. The priests of Ba'al encouraged every kind of foolishness—all in the name of gods and goddesses that did not exist.

▶ Read **1 Kings 18:19–40** and select the best answer to each question.

   ◉ **Verse 19 – Of the 850 false prophets that Jezebel supported, how many served Ba'al?**
    ☐ 400   ☐ 450   ☐ 700

   ◉ **Verse 21 – What two choices did Elijah present to the Israelites?**
    ☐ Worship God or Ba'al   ☐ Follow King Ahab or Elijah   ☐ Fire or water

   ◉ **Verse 24 – In this test, how would the true God reveal Himself?**
    ☐ By answering with fire   ☐ By speaking out loud   ☐ By letting it rain

- ◉ **Verses 26–29 – To get Ba'al to answer, what did the false prophets *not* do?**
  ☐ Cut themselves   ☐ Go around the altar   ☐ Bow down

- ◉ **Verses 30–31 – After asking the people to come near, what did Elijah do first?**
  ☐ Repaired God's altar with 12 stones   ☐ Prayed   ☐ Killed the false prophets

- ◉ **Verses 32–35 – What unusual thing did Elijah do for his burnt offering?**
  ☐ Stood on it   ☐ Used the altar built for Ba'al   ☐ Soaked it with water three times

- ◉ **Verse 37 – Why did Elijah want God to answer?**
  ☐ So the prophets of Ba'al would understand their foolishness
  ☐ So Ahab and Jezebel would be killed
  ☐ So the people would know their God and turn to Him

- ◉ **Verse 38 – How did God respond to Elijah's prayer?**
  ☐ By sending fire to consume the offering, altar, and the water
  ☐ By sending fire to kill all the prophets of Ba'al
  ☐ By sending fire to destroy everyone who had worshiped Ba'al

- ◉ **Verse 39 – When God proved Himself, how did the people of Israel respond?**
  ☐ They mocked Elijah and said he was trying to trick them.
  ☐ They fell down and declared that the Lord is God.
  ☐ They ate all the offerings.

- ◉ **Verse 40 – What did Elijah and the people do to the prophets of Ba'al?**
  ☐ Executed them   ☐ Sent them back to Sidon   ☐ Imprisoned them

▶ Finally, read **1 Kings 19:1–2**. After all this, what did Jezebel do?

____

Winning Your Race

Foolish people will refuse to see the truth even if it's right in front of them. This kind of foolishness becomes a bigger problem when we pass it on to others.

▶ Just about everyone can be a leader to someone. Think about the people in your life that notice what you say and do. How could they be harmed by foolish decisions you might make?

____

____

____

____

____

Greed and Envy

<table>
<tr><td colspan="2" align="center">Vocabulary</td></tr>
<tr><td>• Greed – A desire for more than what is good or needed; the opposite of gratitude</td></tr>
<tr><td>• Envy / Coveting – Wanting something that another person has, even if it's sinful to take</td></tr>
<tr><td>• Fasting – Choosing not to eat, often to focus on praying or some other spiritual activity</td></tr>
<tr><td>• Sackcloth – Rough fabric used for sacks or bags; in Scripture, often worn to show sadness</td></tr>
<tr><td>• Contentment – Peace and gratitude for what we already have; happiness in our current state</td></tr>
</table>

16-A Naboth's Vineyard

Ahab and Jezebel were foolish not just because they worshiped false gods. Like many other fools, they also worshiped their own desires.

▶ Read **1 Kings 21:1–16** and fill in the blanks.

A man named _________________ had a _____________________ in the city of Jezreel, right next to Ahab's palace. One day, Ahab asked the man to give him the land, or at least sell it to him. But Naboth did not want to give away the _____________________ that his family had left him.

Because he could not have the piece of land, Ahab felt _____________________ and _____________________. He lay on his ___________ and refused to eat.

Jezebel came and asked Ahab why he was so upset. When Ahab told her about Naboth, Jezebel asked him if he really ruled over _______________. She said that she would give Ahab the _____________________ herself.

So Jezebel wrote _____________________ in _________________'s name to the leaders of Naboth's city. The queen ordered them to proclaim a _________________________ and set _____________________ in an important place where everyone could see him. Then two men were to say that he _______________________ both ___________ and the ___________. After that, the leaders would take Naboth and _________________ him to death.

Jezebel's plan went exactly as she had written it. As soon as Jezebel heard that Naboth was _______________, she told Ahab to take the _______________________ for his own.

▶ How should Ahab have responded to Naboth's refusal?

____

____

▶ Do you think Ahab was responsible for Jezebel's crime? Why or why not?

____

____

____

16-B The End of Ahab and Jezebel

▶ God sent Elijah to deliver a message to Ahab. Read **1 Kings 21:17–29** and mark the correct ending to the following sentences.

Verse 19: Because of Ahab's sin, God said that the king would . . .

☐ need to give the vineyard back.	☐ die with his blood falling near Naboth's.	☐ have to work in the vineyard himself.

Verse 22: God promised to cut off Ahab because he had made . . .

☐ several mistakes.	☐ Israel sin.	☐ a new religion.

Verse 23: God also promised that Jezebel would . . .

☐ pay Naboth's family.	☐ rule in Ahab's place.	☐ be eaten by dogs.

Verse 27: Ahab responded to God's message by tearing his clothes, . . .

☐ making *sackcloth*, and being sad.	☐ eating *sackcloth*, and being sad.	☐ wearing *sackcloth*, fasting, and being sad.

Verse 29: Because Ahab humbled himself, God decided . . .

☐ to delay the punishment.	☐ not to punish anyone.	☐ to punish only Jezebel.

▶ Look again at these verses from **1 Kings 21**. How did Elijah describe Ahab's sin?

- ⊙ **Verse 20 –** ____

  ____

- ⊙ **Verse 22 –** ____

  ____

- ⊙ **Verse 26 –** ____

▶ Ahab later went to war against Syria, and he tried to protect himself by wearing a disguise. Read **1 Kings 22:34–40**. What happened to the king?

____

____

Jezebel did not escape God's justice, either. She was later betrayed and killed by the Israelites, and her body was eaten by dogs. Ahab and Jezebel's reign ended in shame.

16-C The Sin of Coveting

▶ Look again at the definitions for **greed**, **envy**, and **coveting** on page 75. Explain how Ahab was an example of these words.

Greed	_____________________________________ _____________________________________ _____________________________________
Envy / Coveting	_____________________________________ _____________________________________ _____________________________________

▶ Jesus told a parable about greed in **Luke 12:13–21**. Read the passage and answer the following.

- ⊙ What made the rich man feel secure and happy?

  ____

  ____

- ⊙ In your own words, what point did Jesus make through this story? (vv. 15, 20–21)

  ____

  ____

  ____

It's not always wrong to want things. But we have to examine our desires and ask if they lead us toward good or bad. Do we want what God wants for us?

If we expect people or stuff to give us true joy, we've begun to make an idol. We may not worship statues like Ahab and Jezebel did, but we shouldn't put anything in God's place. We must value Him first, and we must depend on Him. Only He can give us joy.

► Finally, read **1 Timothy 6:6–10** and answer the questions below.

⊙ What is great gain? ____

⊙ What does the love of wealth tempt people to do? (v. 10)

____

____

Winning Your Race

► In the spaces below, write a couple of the things you wish you had. Then take some time to think about the blessings that God has already given you.

⊙ I wish that ____

____,

but I am thankful that _______________________________________

____.

⊙ I wish that ____

____,

but I am thankful that _______________________________________

____.

Enemies of God

Vocabulary

- **Satan** – An evil being opposed to God and those who follow Him; means "adversary"

- **Devil** – Another name for Satan; means "liar" or "deceiver"

- **Carnal** – Relating to physical desires and appetites; often relating to sinful pleasure

- **The World** – In Scripture, can mean the system of power built by those who oppose God

- **Trespass / Transgress** – To step over a line or boundary; to break a rule

17-A Satan

Scripture describes three forces that oppose God: Satan, our human desires, and the world system. We'll look at passages that describe each enemy, beginning with the Father of Lies, Satan.

▶ Read the passages and briefly describe what Satan does in each.

Passage	What does Satan do?
Job 1:6–7	
John 8:42–45	
Acts 5:3	
Hebrews 2:9, 14–15	

Passage	What does Satan do?
1 Peter 5:8–9	
Revelation 12:9	

▶ Satan would accomplish little if he always appeared as a giant monster. Read what Paul wrote in **2 Corinthians 11:13–15**.

⊙ What do Satan's followers sometimes look like? (vv. 13, 15)

____

⊙ How can Satan appear? (v. 14) _______________________

▶ Satan is strong and cunning, but he cannot come close to the power of God. Read what Jesus said in **Matthew 25:41**. What has God prepared for Satan and his followers?

____

Satan cannot truly challenge God, but he pushes many people in the world toward evil. We could not understand everything about the devil, but Scripture has given us what we need to know for now.

▶ Read **James 4:7**. What two things does James say to do?

____

____

17-B The Flesh

Satan is not the only wicked being in the universe. He can tempt us to do evil, but evil is only tempting because part of us wants it. Since Adam and Eve, humans have naturally desired to turn from God toward sin. Scripture calls these sinful desires "the flesh."

▶ Paul wrote about this in the Book of Romans. Read the passages and complete the summaries.

Romans 7:18	I know that there is no _________________ dwelling in my flesh (sinful nature).
Romans 7:19	I do not do the _________________ I want to do. Instead, I do the _____________ that I would rather not do.

Romans 8:6	The **carnal**, fleshly mind is _________________, but a Spirit-filled mind has _____________ and _________________.
Romans 8:7	The mind focused on the flesh is _________________________________ God. It will not and cannot follow His Law.
Romans 8:8	People living in the flesh cannot _________________________________.

▶ In **Galatians 5:19–21**, Paul describes some of the behaviors of people who give in to their sinful desires. List just four of these sins below.

____

____

▶ Note **verse 21** again. What is true about everyone who stays chained to these sins?

____

▶ Given what you read in Galatians 5, mark each statement below as true or false.

People in the flesh usually show self-control.	☐ True	☐ False
People in the flesh stir up unnecessary conflict with others.	☐ True	☐ False
People in the flesh usually show love to other people.	☐ True	☐ False
People in the flesh want to fulfill their own desires no matter what.	☐ True	☐ False
People in the flesh treat other people like tools, toys, or just objects.	☐ True	☐ False
People in the flesh can follow and please God.	☐ True	☐ False

17-C The World System

One flesh-focused person is bad enough, but we live on a planet filled with sinful people. These people gather together to create nations, governments, companies, and other kinds of groups. Just like individual people, these groups can naturally oppose God. Scripture calls this entire system "the world."

▶ Match the following passages to what they teach about the world. Complete the summaries by filling in the blanks. The first letter is given for you.

A. 1 Corinthians 1:20	B. Ephesians 2:1–2	C. Ephesians 6:11–12	D. James 4:4	E. 1 John 2:16	F. 1 John 2:17

	Truth About the World
A	God has turned the _______________________ of the world into foolishness.
	All believers used to be dead in their _______________________ and sin— back when we behaved like the world and Satan wanted.
	The _______________ of the flesh, the _______________ of the eyes, and the _______________ of life are all from the world, not God.
	Christians do not struggle against _______________ and _______________, but against evil spiritual forces.
	_______________________ with the world makes us oppose God.
	The world and its sinful desires pass away, but the person who does God's will _______________________ forever.

Winning Your Race

▶ What is the difference between loving the world system and loving people *in* the world?

____

____

____

____

____

► Any good desire can be corrupted into something bad. In the space below, describe three good desires and how they could become sinful.

It's good to want . . .	**But I would sin if I . . .**

It's good to want . . .	**But I would sin if I . . .**

It's good to want . . .	**But I would sin if I . . .**

How We Sin

Vocabulary

- **Temptation** – The act of tempting; any pressure to do wrong; can refer to the thing that tempts

- **The Fall** – Humanity's turn from God toward sin and death; the results of the first sin

- **Manna** – A bread-like food that God gave Israel in the wilderness

18-A Eve and the Serpent

We sin when we give in to **temptation** and disobey God. We can find the first example of temptation in Genesis 3.

▶ Read **Genesis 2:15–17**. What one rule did God give the very first humans?

____

____

▶ Read how the serpent tempted Eve in **Genesis 3:1–6**. Answer the following questions.

  ⊙ What did the serpent question first? (v. 1)

  ____

  ⊙ Eve repeated God's command, but what did she add to it? (v. 3)

  ____

  ⊙ The serpent tried to get Eve to doubt God's words. What did the serpent say would happen if she ate the fruit? (vv. 4–5)

    1. She would not _______________.

    2. Instead, her eyes would be _______________________.

    3. She would become like _________________.

    4. She would know _________________ and _____________.

◉ What do you think the serpent's words were?

◻ Truth ◻ Lies ◻ A mix of truth and lies

◉ Why did Eve choose to eat the fruit? (v. 6)

____

____

____

____

◉ Who else ate it? ____________________________

◉ Why do you think he made this choice?

____

____

____

____

► God judged Adam and Eve for their sin. Read what happened in **Genesis 3:16–24**. What was the big lie within the serpent's words?

____

► Finally, read **Romans 5:12**. What was the main result of the first sin? We call this *the Fall*.

____

____

18-B Sin and God's Law

Adam and Eve had just one rule to break, but now we know that there are many ways to sin. So many things can tempt us to turn away from God. God therefore gave Israel the Law to teach them about the things they should not do.

► Read **1 John 3:4–8** and fill in the blanks to complete the summaries.

Verse 4	Whoever sins ____.
Verse 5	But Jesus came to Earth to take away ________________. In Him is no sin.
Verse 6	No one who ________________ in Christ will keep on sinning.
Verse 8	Those who continue sinning are of the ________________. He has been sinning from the beginning, but the Son of God appeared to destroy this work.

► Continue reading **1 John 3:9–12** and answer the following questions.

  ⊙ How do God's children show that they don't follow the devil? (vv. 9–10)

  ____

  ____

  ____

  ⊙ What message have we had since the very beginning? (v. 11)

  ____

► In verse 12, the writer mentions Cain, the first son of Adam and Eve. Read about what Cain did in **Genesis 4:1–12**.

  ⊙ When Cain was upset, God talked to him. To avoid sin, what did Cain need to do? (v. 7)

  ____

  ____

  ⊙ Did Cain follow God's warning?　☐ Yes　☐ No

► Unlike Eve, Cain didn't sin right after talking to a lying serpent. Based on everything you just read, what do you think led Cain to sin?

  ____

  ____

  ____

18-C Jesus' Response to Temptation

At the beginning of Jesus' earthly ministry, He spent forty days in the wilderness with the Holy Spirit. He ate nothing and saw no one else, but then Satan came to tempt Him. As God, Jesus did not sin, but the devil tried to put pressure on Him.

► How did Jesus handle temptation? Read **Luke 4:1–13** and complete the following summaries.

	Satan tempted Jesus to . . .	Jesus responded with . . .
Verses 3–4	Turn a _________________ into _________________	Man does not live _________________ _________________. (Deut. 8:3)
Verses 5–8	_________________ him	You should _________________ and serve only _________________. (Deut. 6:13)
Verses 9–12	Jump off the _________________ to be saved by _________________	You should not _________________ the Lord your God. (Deut. 6:16)

► Throughout their conversation, both Satan and Jesus quoted Scripture from the Old Testament. Does that mean they were both right? Why or why not?

____

____

____

► Read what Moses told Israel in **Deuteronomy 8:2–3**. Why did God feed the people *manna* in the wilderness?

____

____

____

► How can we avoid being tricked by people that quote Scripture in a wrong way?

____

____

____

____

Winning Your Race

► Jesus left us the story of His temptation for a reason. What do you think we can learn from His example? He is much wiser and stronger than us, but how can we imitate Him?

____

____

____

____

► We often sin when we're tired, sad, or struggling with doubt. But when we face temptation, we should remind ourselves about who God is and what He does for us. List two truths about God that you can remember when tempted to sin.

  ◉ ____

____

  ◉ ____

____

Overcoming Temptation

19-A Peter's Denial

▶ The day before Jesus was crucified, Simon Peter faced an important test. Read **Luke 22:31–34, 54–62** and mark the following statements as true or false. For each false statement, rewrite it correctly.

Verses 31–32: Satan wanted permission to "sift" Peter like wheat, but Jesus prayed that Peter's faith would not fail. ☐ True ☐ False

Correction: ____

____

Verse 33: Peter knew that he would reject Jesus one day. ☐ True ☐ False

Correction: ____

____

Verse 54: When Jesus was arrested, Peter ran away to hide with the other disciples. ☐ True ☐ False

Correction: ____

____

Verses 55–56: As Peter sat by a fire near the high priest's house, a servant recognized him as a follower of Jesus. ☐ True ☐ False

Correction: ____

____

<table>
<tr><td>Verses 56–60: While at the fire, Peter denied Jesus three times.</td><td>☐ True ☐ False</td></tr>
</table>

Correction: ____

____

<table>
<tr><td>Verses 61–62: When Peter realized what he had done, he considered it a small mistake.</td><td>☐ True ☐ False</td></tr>
</table>

Correction: ____

____

____

To overcome temptation, we must realize that we are not immune to sin. Because of this test, Peter understood that even he could bow to fear. No one is perfect, and we all need the strength of Christ to overcome temptation.

▶ Thankfully, this was not the end of Peter's story. After Jesus' death and resurrection, He appeared to the disciples on the shore of Galilee. Read **John 21:7–17** and answer the following questions.

◉ What did Peter do when he realized it was Jesus? (v. 7)

____

◉ After Jesus offered breakfast to the disciples, what did He ask Peter? (v. 15)

____

◉ How did Peter answer?　　☐ Yes ☐ No

◉ What do you think Jesus meant by the command He kept repeating? (vv. 15–17) What did He want Peter to do? Remember Jesus' prayer in **Luke 22:32**.

____

____

____

◉ Do you think that Jesus forgave Peter?　　☐ Yes ☐ No

Why or why not? ____

____

____

Peter had betrayed Jesus, but he did not give up. He worked hard to share the gospel. Peter wasn't perfect, but he spent his life following Jesus and caring for His "sheep."

► God has given us much Scripture to help us understand and resist temptation. Read the following passages and complete the summaries.

Galatians 6:1	When helping someone stuck in sin, we should be careful in case we are also _______________________.
1 Corinthians 10:13	Others have faced temptations like ours. God is _______________________ and will not allow us to be tempted more than we're able to stand. For every temptation, God has given us a way to _______________________.
James 1:2–3	Temptations test our faith to produce _______________________.
James 1:13–15	_______________________ does not tempt anyone. Instead, people are tempted when they are carried off by their own _______________________.
James 4:7	The devil will flee us if we _______________________ him.
Hebrews 4:15	Jesus is a high priest who understands our weakness. He was tempted just like we are, but without _______________________.

To Satan, temptation is a way to convince us to do wrong. But to God, temptation is a test of our faith. Do we trust that He cares for us? Do we trust that His commands are good for us? God does not want us to sin, but He allows us to be tested so that we can learn to trust Him more. Thankfully, He offers help whenever we ask.

► But what happens when we give in to temptation? Read **2 Corinthians 7:9–12** again. Remember that Paul had corrected some serious sins in the Corinthian church.

- Why did Paul rejoice for the Corinthian believers? (v. 9)
  ☐ They were sad.　　☐ They had sinned.　　☐ Their sadness led to repentance.

- In this passage, Paul describes two kinds of sorrow or grief—the worldly kind and the godly kind. What is the difference between these two?

____

____

____

____

19-C The Armor of God

How can we defend against Satan's attacks? What tools has God given us?

► The Apostle Paul wrote about this in **Ephesians 6:10–18**. Read the passage and label the picture below. To stand against evil, we must rely on . . .

Verse 17 – ______________________________________
____

Verse 14 – ______________________________________
____

Verse 14 – ______________________________________
____

Verse 17 – ______________________________________
____

Verse 16 – ______________________________________
____

Verse 15 – ______________________________________
____

► Review the passages and answer the following questions.

◉ Where does our strength come from? (vv. 10–11)

____

◉ What is the point of all this armor? (v. 13)

☐ To help us look better than other people
☐ To help us prove to unbelievers that they're wrong
☐ To help us stand against the devil's trickery

◉ What should we be doing continually? (v. 18)

____

Winning Your Race

There's no simple way to overcome temptation, but here are a few principles:

- ◉ Like Jesus, we should live by God's Word.
- ◉ Like Peter and the Corinthian believers, we should turn from any sins we already know about. We should follow our guilt to repentance.
- ◉ We should build up our armor by seeking God's truth. We should study the Word and listen to mature Christians.
- ◉ We should stay alert for temptation. We should resist it with prayer and the Word.

► Think about how often you pray for help during temptation. Ask God to help you remember Him and His Word whenever you're tempted to sin.

► Consider the situation below and write your response.

Your friend Greg says he has a classmate named Josh that just won't leave him alone. Josh keeps following Greg around, asking questions and making jokes. Greg can't stand it. The other day, Josh accidentally bumped into Greg. Greg snapped and pushed him back—not very hard, but Josh did fall down. Greg didn't mean to hurt anyone, and he feels bad.

◉ If Greg asked you for advice, what would you say?

____

____

____

____

____

____

____

____

Conformed to His Image

Vocabulary

- **Temple** – A holy or sacred place for worship
- **Ambassador** – A messenger or representative; someone who represents another
- **Reconciliation** – The act of reconciling; restoring a good relationship

20-A A New Person

As you may remember from Lesson 5, God saves us so that we can glorify Him, follow Him, and become like His Son, Jesus. When we place our trust in Christ, God begins to transform us.

▶ Shortly before His death, Jesus told His disciples that He would soon leave them. He gave them some final encouragement and instruction. Read **John 13:33–35** and answer the following.

- ◉ After Jesus rose again, He would ascend into heaven. Could the disciples follow Him yet?
  ☐ Yes ☐ No

- ◉ What command did He give them? (v. 34)

  ____

- ◉ If they obeyed Him, what would they show others? (v. 35)

  ____

▶ If we have placed our trust in Christ, then He has raised us to a new life in God. Read what Paul wrote about this new life in **Colossians 3:1–17**. Answer the following questions.

- ◉ If Christ has raised us, what should we focus on? (vv. 1–2)

  ____

- ◉ If we've put off our old selves, what is happening to the *new* us? (vv. 9–10)

  ____

  ____

Remember that *disciple* means "student." If we are disciples of Christ, we will study His truth, and He will transform us through what we learn.

▶ We should reflect Jesus to others. So what should disciples put off, and what should we put on? In each box below, list at least five behaviors.

Colossians 3:5, 8–9 . . .	Colossians 3:12–16
We should *put off* _______________________	We should *put on* _______________________

Every sin is a weight that keeps us from running and enjoying the race that God has set for us. We put aside these old things while putting on truth and love.

▶ How would you write the message of **Colossians 3:17** in your own words?

20-B Temple of the Spirit

When we decide to trust Jesus as our Savior and as our Lord, we begin to change. The Holy Spirit lives inside us, and every part of us belongs to God. Through us, God shows His love to other people.

▶ Read **1 Corinthians 6:19–20** and answer the following questions.

◉ How is a Christian's body like a temple?

____

◉ Why are we not our own? Why do we belong to God?

____

◉ What do you think Paul means by "price"?

____

____

◉ What should we do with our bodies—and everything else? _______________________________

Jesus expects His followers to represent Him well, but we don't have to do this on our own. God's Spirit will help us live out His teaching.

▶ What does the Spirit do for believers? Read the following passages and complete the summaries.

John 14:26	Jesus promised that the Spirit would _______________ the disciples all things and help them remember everything Jesus _______________ to them.
John 15:26–27	Jesus promised that this Spirit of Truth would _______________ about Him.
Romans 8:26	The Spirit helps us in our weakness. Since we don't know how to pray, the Spirit _______________ for us with groans that cannot be spoken.
1 Corinthians 2:12–14	The Spirit helps us _______________ the things that God freely gave to us. We cannot interpret His Word without Him.
2 Timothy 1:13–14	The Spirit can help us _______________ the good teaching that others passed on to us.

▶ Do you ask the Spirit for help with the things above? Consider taking a moment to pray and make more room in your "temple" for Him.

20-C Ambassador of Christ

As Jesus' disciples, we represent Him to the world. People cannot see Jesus face to face right now, but people *can* see His followers. It is our mission to reflect Jesus by our words and actions.

▶ Read **2 Corinthians 5:14–21** and mark the best answer to the following questions.

- **What does it mean to be "dead" with Christ? (vv. 14–15)**
  ☐ We now live for ourselves. ☐ We now live for Christ. ☐ We can do nothing.

- **What did God do through Christ? (v. 18)**
  ☐ Reconciled us to Himself ☐ Abandoned us ☐ Changed how we look

- **How did Paul perform God's ministry of reconciliation? (vv. 18–20)**
  ☐ By condemning people under the Old Testament Law
  ☐ By telling people that there was no way to know God
  ☐ By begging people to be reconciled to God

- **What can we be for Christ? (v. 20)**
  ☐ Kings and queens ☐ Ambassadors ☐ Forerunners

- **For us to become the righteousness of God, what did Christ become? (v. 21)**
  ☐ A rock ☐ An ambassador ☐ Sin

Winning Your Race

▶ Write a short story about someone being an ambassador for Christ. Describe how your main character would respond to a challenge in a Christlike way. Use one of the following challenges, or make up your own.

- Another student needs help completing a project.

- Someone gets hurt in the gym.

- A group of friends mocks someone harshly for making a mistake.

- Your main character has too much schoolwork to do.

- Your main character has to present a huge report tomorrow.

____

____

____

____

____

____

Vocabulary

- **Conscience** – Inner feelings of right or wrong; our moral sense

- **Leaven / Yeast** – A single-cell fungus used in breadmaking to help the dough rise

21-A Division or Unity

In previous lessons, you read some of Paul's instructions for the Corinthian believers. These Christians lived in a terribly wicked city, and many believers were stuck in the world's ways. For this lesson, we'll look at some of the problems within the church at Corinth and how we can avoid these same problems today.

▶ Read **1 Corinthians 1:10–17** and answer the following questions.

◉ What had Paul heard about the church through Chloe's household? (vv. 10–11)

____

◉ What caused this problem? (vv. 12–13)

____

____

▶ Paul grieved over the problems in Corinth because he had spent time serving there. Read ahead in **1 Corinthians 2:1–5**.

◉ How did Paul *not* preach the gospel in Corinth?

____

____

◉ Instead, how *did* Paul speak to the Corinthians?

____

____

◉ Why did Paul let people see his weaknesses instead of boasting over his strengths? (vv. 4–5)

____

____

▶ Read **1 Corinthians 3:1–9** and mark the following statements as true or false. Write the numbers of the verses that helped you decide.

Statement	True or False?		Verses
Paul taught the Corinthians with "milk" because they were mostly mature believers.	☐ True	☐ False	
Christ "planted" the seeds of truth, Apollos "watered" them, and Paul caused everything to grow.	☐ True	☐ False	
Paul and Apollos were not as important as the Lord who gave them their tasks.	☐ True	☐ False	
When the Corinthian believers acted selfishly and fought, they were acting like people without Jesus.	☐ True	☐ False	
The Corinthian believers were now ready for more difficult teaching.	☐ True	☐ False	
God deserves the credit for everything good in a church. This is all His work.	☐ True	☐ False	

21-B Sin and Conscience

There is a spiritual side to us as well as a physical side. Some Corinthian believers thought that since their spirits would go to heaven one day, they could do whatever they wanted with their bodies. One man in the church lived in terrible sin—even worse than the Corinthian unbelievers. Instead of correcting or removing this man from the church, the church leaders became arrogant and proud.

▶ Paul told the Corinthians to put this man out of the assembly. Read **1 Corinthians 5:6–8** and complete the summaries.

Verse 6	Paul asked if they knew that a little ______________________ can spread through the whole piece of dough.
Verse 7	The Corinthian believers needed to ______________________________ the old sins so that the church could honor Christ.
Verse 8	A group of believers should not be leavened with ______________________ and ______________________________, but instead have ______________________ and ______________________.

► Continue reading in **1 Corinthians 5:9–13** and answer the following.

⊙ Paul did not want the believers to be close to people who kept committing terrible sins. But if Christians couldn't be around anyone like that, what would they have to do? (vv. 9–10)

____

⊙ So what did Paul mean? Who should believers not accompany? (v. 11)

____

____

When we take the name "Christian," we should not continue dishonoring Christ. If someone in the church makes a habit of sin without repenting, the church should not allow that sin to spread and harm more people. The leaders of the church should speak up and show the right way.

► There was another issue creating problems. Read **1 Corinthians 8:4–13**.

⊙ What kind of food were some believers eating? (v. 4)

____

⊙ Were these gods real? Did they have any power? (vv. 4–6) ☐ Yes ☐ No

⊙ Did some people think these gods were real? (v. 7) ☐ Yes ☐ No

⊙ Was there anything wrong with the food itself? (v. 8) ☐ Yes ☐ No

► But some believers had a sensitive conscience. If they ate the food, they might feel like they were being pulled back into idolatry. To help these people, what did Paul encourage the Corinthians to do? Summarize his advice in **verses 9–13**.

____

____

____

____

____

____

► Can you think of another harmless thing that can become sinful if it hurts someone's conscience?

____

____

____

____

21-C Using Our Gifts

God saves all kinds of people from all kinds of backgrounds. The church in Corinth had men and women, Jews and Greeks, even slaves and free citizens. Only Jesus could bring these people together to work for good.

Many Corinthian believers had special jobs, talents, or skills. But instead of being grateful, some thought that their gifts made them *better*. They thought that God valued some parts of His church more than others.

▶ Read about this problem in **1 Corinthians 12:12–31** and mark the correct ending to each sentence.

Verse 12: To help believers understand, Paul pictured the Church as a . . .

| ☐ gigantic temple. | ☐ butterfly. | ☐ human body. |

Verse 13: The Church is unified because we have one . . .

| ☐ founder, Paul himself. | ☐ Spirit. | ☐ uniform to wear. |

Verse 17: If a body were made completely out of eyes, how could we . . .

| ☐ see? | ☐ hear? | ☐ fly into space? |

Verse 18: God designed the Church body . . .

| ☐ exactly how He wanted. | ☐ to make us all look good. | ☐ so we could try doing everything at least once. |

Verses 22–24: Parts that seem weak or less honorable should be given . . .

| ☐ discipline. | ☐ mockery. | ☐ great respect. |

Verses 25–26: If a church has unity, all the believers will suffer if . . .

| ☐ they have been rejoicing for too long. | ☐ one believer is honored, and they will rejoice if one suffers. | ☐ one believer suffers, and they will rejoice if one is honored. |

▶ In **verses 27–31**, Paul mentions different kinds of spiritual gifts in the early Church. Why do you think believers have different skills, talents, or abilities?

____

____

____

____

Winning Your Race

▶ What are some things you're good at doing?

____

____

____

▶ What are some things you're not so good at doing—at least not yet?

____

____

____

▶ What skills do you want to improve?

____

____

▶ Think about how your gifts might be used in the spiritual activities listed below. Mark the two that best match your gifts—or might match one day, as you improve.

    ☐ Teaching and explaining truth from God's Word

    ☐ Serving others' physical needs

    ☐ Encouraging people and praying for them

    ☐ Giving helpful things to others

    ☐ Leading and organizing people

    ☐ Reaching out to people who face difficult challenges

▶ Pick one of the activities above, and explain how you might be able to help with this even now.

____

____

____

____

The Lamb of God

Vocabulary

- **Passover** – A Jewish holiday celebrating the day God rescued the Israelites from Egypt

- **Plague** – A disaster for a large number of people; in Scripture, often reveals God's judgment

- **Stricken** – Struck or beaten; suffering under violent abuse

- **Iniquity** – A wicked or evil action; a sin

- **Propitiation** – A sacrifice made to atone or set things right

22-A Sin and Sacrifice

You may remember that Jesus visited John the Baptist early in His ministry. Jesus traveled to Bethany near the Jordan River, and He asked John to baptize Him.

▶ Read **John 1:24–31** and answer the following questions.

◉ John was the forerunner of the Messiah. What did John feel unworthy to do for Jesus? (v. 27)

____

◉ What did John call Jesus? (v. 29)

____

◉ What did John say that Jesus would do? (v. 29)

____

By describing Jesus in this way, John tried to show Jesus' importance. John was prophesying about Jesus' death for our sins.

Early in the Book of Genesis, we read that God expected sacrifices from those who followed Him. People offered sacrifices to show different things—like gratitude for harvests or sorrow over sin. The sacrifices might include animals, grain, or other valuables.

► God told Abraham, the father of Israel, to make a very unusual sacrifice. Read **Genesis 22:1–18** and match each sentence to its best ending.

	God commanded Abraham to take his only son Isaac and . . .	**A.**	offer him on a mountain in Moriah.
	After three days' travel, Abraham told his servants that he and Isaac would . . .	**B.**	call the place *Jehovahjireh*, meaning "the Lord will provide."
	When Isaac asked about a lamb, Abraham said that God would . . .	**C.**	take his knife and make the sacrifice.
	After binding Isaac on top of the altar, Abraham reached out to . . .	**D.**	go worship on the mountain and then come back.
	According to the angel, God knew that Abraham had chosen to . . .	**E.**	fear Him and not withhold Isaac.
	After being stopped by the angel, Abraham looked up to . . .	**F.**	see a ram caught in a thicket.
	Because of the replacement sacrifice, Abraham chose to . . .	**G.**	provide one for the burnt offering.

God tested Abraham's faith by asking him to sacrifice his son. Isaac was not killed that day, but he was still sacrificed. Isaac and all his descendants belonged to God. And through this special nation, God sent His own Son as a sacrifice for the world.

► How is the ram of Genesis 22 like Jesus?

____

____

____

____

22-B The Passover Lamb

Centuries after Abraham, the Israelites had grown into a huge nation, but they were bound as slaves in Egypt. God sent Moses to free them, and with Moses came ten **plagues** to judge the Egyptians. During the plagues, the Pharaoh of Egypt kept promising to let the Israelites go, but then he would harden his heart and refuse.

The tenth plague was the worst of all. God sent an angel of death to kill all the firstborn in Egypt. But before He did, He told His people how they could avoid this disaster.

▶ Read **Exodus 12:1–6** and answer the following questions.

⊙ The Hebrews marked this event on their new calendar. On what day would it begin? (vv. 2–3)

____

Jews today call this month *Nisan*, and it falls across March and April on modern calendars.

⊙ What kind of sacrifice would the Hebrews prepare and eat? (vv. 4–5)

____

▶ Continue reading in **Exodus 12:7–11** and answer the following questions by drawing pictures.

Where did they place the blood of the sacrifice?	How did they cook the meat?

What else did they eat with the meat?	How did they eat their meal?

By doing these things, the Israelites marked themselves as separate from the Egyptians. They showed faith in God by readying themselves to leave.

▶ Read the following verses in **Exodus 12** and answer the questions.

⊙ **Verse 17** – What would Israel call this feast?

____

⊙ **Verses 26–27** – Many years later, when children asked about this practice, what would their parents tell them?

____

____

____

22-C Our Sacrificial Lamb

In the Old Testament Law, God explained how His priests could offer sacrifices to honor Him. By following careful rituals, the people of Israel could show their repentance, their faith, and their awe for God.

Animal sacrifices also revealed the cost of sin. Their purpose was holy, so the animals needed to be perfect and spotless.

▶ The prophet Isaiah wrote about the One who would save Israel. Read **Isaiah 53:4–10** and answer the following questions.

⊙ This Person would be sent by God, but God would also make Him suffer. What does Isaiah compare this Person to? (v. 7)

____

⊙ Does He deserve to be treated this way? (v. 9)   ☐ Yes   ☐ No

⊙ In your own words, why does this Person suffer? (vv. 4–6, 10)

____

____

The Gospel writers identified this person as Jesus Christ. They described how He fulfilled these words when He willingly died on the cross.

▶ Note the definition for **_propitiation_** on page 103 and then read **1 John 4:9–10**. In your own words, why did Jesus choose to die?

____

____

____

► Read **Hebrews 10:1–18** and complete the summaries.

Verses 1–2	The Old Testament sacrifices offered every ________________ could not make people perfect. Otherwise, they could have stopped offering sacrifices.
Verse 3	Instead, these sacrifices were a ____________________________________ of sins every year.
Verse 4	The ____________________ of these animals cannot take away ______________.
Verses 5–9	God the Father took no pleasure in these sacrifices for their own sake, so He sent Jesus into the world to accomplish His will.
Verse 10	By God's will, we have been sanctified by the offering of Jesus' ______________. This sacrifice was made just once for all time.
Verses 15–16	God now puts His ________________ in our hearts and writes them in our minds.
Verse 17	He chooses to remember our ____ no longer.
Verse 18	Where there is forgiveness for sin, there is no more ____________________ for sin.

Winning Your Race

► If God knows everything, how do you think **Hebrews 10:17** could be true?

____

____

____

____

► If you've trusted Jesus to be the propitiation for your sins, you live in God's love and forgiveness. Believers don't have to offer sacrifices for sin. Why then do Christians still sacrifice their time and effort for God?

____

____

____

The Miracles of Jesus

23-A Types of Miracles

God used miracles throughout the Bible for many different reasons:

- To show His power so that people would hear and believe Him
- To help people and encourage their trust in Him
- To judge sin and challenge people to repent

When Jesus Christ served on Earth, He also used miracles to reach out to the people around Him. The four Gospels—Matthew, Mark, Luke, and John—together record more than forty miracles of Jesus.

▶ Read about one of these miracles in **Luke 17:11–19** and answer the following questions.

- Walking to Jerusalem, Jesus met ten men who had *leprosy*. What did they say to Him? (v. 13)

____

- What did He tell them to do? (v. 14)

____

- When they did what Jesus said, was their faith rewarded? ☐ Yes ☐ No

- What did one man do that the other nine didn't? (vv. 15–18)

____

► Jesus' miracles revealed His power over spiritual things as well as physical. Read each passage below and complete the summaries.

Matthew 8:16	Jesus _________________ out evil spirits from people. He also healed those who were sick.
Matthew 9:18–25	While Jesus was walking, a woman _________________ His clothing and was healed for her faith. Jesus continued on to raise a girl from the dead.
Mark 2:1–12	Jesus told a paralyzed man that his sins were _________________ and that he could now rise and walk.
Luke 8:22–25	During a storm, Jesus _________________ the wind and the raging sea, and there was a sudden calm.
John 6:5–14	Jesus took five _________________ and two _________________ and fed over five thousand people.

23-B Travels in Israel

► Read the following passages and summarize what Jesus did in each passage. Write the location of each event, as well.

Passage	Miracle	Location
Matthew 8:5–13	He healed the _________________'s servant.	**A.** _________________ (**v. 5**)
Matthew 15:29–31	He healed many who were _________________ _________________ _________________.	**B.** Near the _________________ _________________ (**v. 29**)
Mark 6:1–5	He healed only a few _________________ people, but He did no great miracles because of the town's unbelief.	**C.** Jesus' hometown of _________________ (see **Luke 4:16**)
John 2:1–11	He turned water into _________________. This was Jesus' first public miracle.	**D.** _________________ in Galilee (**v. 1**)
John 5:1–9	He healed a lame man near a _________________ called Bethesda.	**E.** _________________ (**v. 1**)

► On the following page is a map of Israel during the time of Christ. Use the **blue letters** above to label the same locations on the map.

► Complete the map by labeling the following locations:

- **The Jordan** – Jesus was baptized in this river. It flows south from the Sea of Galilee.

- **The Dead Sea** – The Jordan ends in this salt-filled lake to the south.

- **The Mediterranean Sea** – This is the large body of water to the west of Israel. On a world map, you can find it between Europe, Africa, and the Middle East.

- **Bethlehem** – This small town was the birthplace of Jesus. The location is marked by a dot just south of Jerusalem.

- **Judea** – During Jesus' ministry, the land was divided into three main regions. Galilee was in the north, Samaria was in the middle, and Judea was in the south around Jerusalem.

23-C Responses to His Miracles

▶ People responded to Jesus' miracles in different ways. Some believed Him, and others rejected Him. Read about one miracle in **John 9:1–7** and answer the following questions.

⊙ Note what the disciples asked in **verse 2**. Why did they think the man had been born blind?

____

⊙ What was the true reason? (v. 3)

____

⊙ Describe what Jesus did to heal the man. (vv. 6–7)

____

____

▶ Continue reading the following verses from **John 9** and note how different people reacted to the man who could now see.

Verses 8–9	The _____________________________ and others wondered if this was really the same blind man who was begging before.
Verses 13–16	The Pharisees were upset that Jesus did not keep the _____________________. They thought that He dishonored the day by healing the man.
Verse 18	The Jewish religious leaders did not believe the man had been _______________ until they talked to his parents.
Verses 31–34	When the man kept insisting that Jesus must have come from _____________, the Pharisees cast him out of the assembly.

At first, many people followed Jesus just to catch a glimpse of His miracles. But as He began to teach more about Himself and His mission, they did not want to accept what He said. Miracles grabbed people's attention, but even the greatest wonders could not create real faith. True believers will trust God even when they cannot see Him.

▶ Read **Hebrews 11:1**. According to this verse, what is faith?

____

____

____

Through science and reason, we can prove some things beyond reasonable doubt—that the Earth is a globe, that humans need oxygen to live, and that *two* plus *two* equals *four*. But there are many things beyond science and reason. For these, we have faith. We need faith to believe that God exists, that He created the universe, and that He loves us.

▶ Thankfully, we don't have to build up faith on our own. Read **Hebrews 12:1–2** and answer the following questions.

⊙ As we run our race, who should we look toward? ________________________

⊙ What has Jesus done for our faith? What is He called in **verse 2**?

____

Winning Your Race

▶ Read about Jesus' miracle in **Matthew 15:32–39** and imagine that you were one of the people in the crowd. In the space below, tell a friend about what you saw. How did Jesus show compassion for the people?

____

____

____

____

____

____

____

____

____

A New Life in Christ

Vocabulary

- **Samaritan** – In Jesus' time, a person from Samaria who descended from both Jews and Gentiles

- **Gentile** – A term for someone who is not Jewish

24-A The Samaritan Woman

▶ Read **John 4:1–5** and complete the following. Check the map on page 110 if you need help.

- ◉ What region was Jesus leaving? (v. 3) **Label it on the map to the right.**

- ◉ What region was He walking toward? (v. 3) **Label it on the map.**

- ◉ What region did He walk through? (v. 4) **Label it on the map.**

- ◉ Near what city or town did He stop? (v. 5) **Label it on the map next to the dot.**

- ◉ Where might Jesus have walked as He traveled from Jerusalem to Cana? **Draw an arrow along the route.**

Jesus did something that many would not have expected from a godly teacher. Most Jews during this time hated the Samaritans and considered them to be corrupt, ungodly traitors to Israel. Some Jews even refused to walk through Samaria, instead choosing to travel along the Jordan. By taking the route directly from Judea to Galilee, Jesus showed that He did not care for such hatred and conflict.

► Continue reading in **John 4:5–15** and fill in the blanks.

When Jesus arrived near Sychar, He was tired from His travels. He decided to rest and sit down at a ______________. A woman came to draw __________________, and Jesus asked her to ________________________ ______________________________. During this time, Jesus' disciples had gone into the town to buy ________________.

The woman could not understand why Jesus would ask her for anything, since He was a __________________ and she was a ________________________________. Jesus said that if she knew who He was, she would ask Him for ________________ water. The woman was confused because Jesus had no way to draw water from the well.

Jesus explained that anyone who drank water from the well would ____________________ again, but those who drank the water He offered would be satisfied forever. This "water" would be a wellspring overflowing to ________________________________. The woman asked Jesus to give her this strange kind of water.

► So Jesus told the woman about her life, showing that He had knowledge from God. He also told her that very soon people could know and worship God in a way like never before. Continue reading the following verses in **John 4** and answer the questions.

◉ **Verse 25** – Who did the woman trust to explain everything some day?

____

◉ **Verse 26** – What did Jesus tell her?

____

◉ **Verses 28–29, 39–42** – What did the woman do? What was the result of this conversation?

____

____

____

24-B The Bread of Life

Jesus helped many people through His miracles, but these wonders were signs of an even greater power. Jesus had come to save people from sin and lead them to a new life with God.

▶ Look again at Jesus' miracle in **John 6:4–15** and order the events below from **1** to **7**.

	Andrew brought a boy with five loaves of bread and two fish.
	Jesus instructed the people to sit down on the ground.
	The people were so excited that they were going to make Jesus a king, but He left them to be alone on a mountain.
	Philip said it would be too expensive to buy food for the crowd, even if everyone ate only a small amount.
	Jesus gave thanks for the food and then distributed it to the people, who took as much as they wanted.
	After the crowd finished eating, there were twelve baskets of food left.
	Jesus tested Philip by asking him where they could buy food for the crowd.

▶ Continue reading in **John 6:16–21**. Later that night, what miracle did Jesus' disciples see?

____

____

▶ The next day, the crowds followed Jesus across the Sea of Galilee and found Him near Capernaum. Continue reading **John 6:25–37** and mark the correct answer to the following questions.

- **According to Jesus, why were the crowds following Him? (v. 26)**
  ☐ Because of His miracles   ☐ Because of the food they ate   ☐ To learn truth

- **What did Jesus say that the crowds should work for? (v. 27)**
  ☐ Food enduring to eternal life   ☐ Food that spoils   ☐ Sugar-free food

- **When asked how to do God's work, what did Jesus say to do? (vv. 28–29)**
  ☐ Be kind   ☐ Conquer sin   ☐ Believe in the Person that God sent

- **Before the people would trust Jesus, what did they want to see? (vv. 30–31)**
  ☐ A sign or miracle   ☐ The fall of the Roman Empire   ☐ God Himself

- **Who alone can give the true bread from heaven? (vv. 32–33)**
  ☐ Moses   ☐ God   ☐ The Pharisees

- **And what is this true bread of life? (v. 35)**
  ☐ Manna   ☐ Jesus Himself   ☐ Unleavened bread for Passover

24-C The Kingdom of Heaven

▶ Read **Matthew 3:2**. What did John the Baptist tell people as he preached?

____

▶ Look again at **Matthew 11:11**. Who did Jesus say would be greater than even John the Baptist?

____

At this time, many Jews were looking for a Messiah to free Israel from the power of the Romans. Like the crowds in John 6, they wanted a king to rule a physical kingdom. They wanted someone to take care of them in earthly ways—to give them food, money, and power.

But John and Jesus taught their disciples about a spiritual kingdom. The true enemy wasn't the Romans, but sin and death. God's Messiah would conquer these spiritual threats and give His followers the greatest gift—eternal life with Him.

▶ While teaching in Galilee, Jesus described how citizens in His kingdom would be different than other people. Instead of natural, sinful attitudes, we need to nurture godly ones. Read the following passages and complete the summaries.

Natural Attitudes	Godly Attitudes
When someone mistreats you, you need to hurt them back.	**Matthew 5:38–42** – Don't ________________ the evil person. Keep showing love even if it costs you.
Hate your enemies.	**Matthew 5:43–44** – ________________ your enemies and ________________ for those who persecute you.
Do good things in front of other people so they'll see and praise you.	**Matthew 6:1–6** – Do good things in secret and receive the best reward, which comes from your ________________.
Gather a lot of wealth and trust your riches to keep you happy.	**Matthew 6:19–21** – Store treasures in ________________, where nothing bad can happen to them.
Who will take care of you? Spend a lot of time worrying about your basic needs.	**Matthew 6:25–34** – Trust God to provide for you as He does for the ________________ and the ________________. Before anything else, seek God's ________________ and His ________________, and He will take care of your needs.

Winning Your Race

► Take a moment to think about your relationship with Christ. How did He save you? How did you become a citizen in His kingdom? In the table below, mark everything that Christians have in common with each other.

☐ We all worship in the same church building.	☐ Christ saved us all by His grace.	☐ Some of us earned our way into the kingdom.
☐ Jesus died for every single one of us.	☐ We're all perfect and sinless beings.	☐ All of us have sinned against God.
☐ Some of us deserve God's love a little more than others do.	☐ Every one of us sins at the same time and in the same ways.	☐ By rising from the dead, Jesus gave us hope for eternal life.

► Read what Jesus prayed to God the Father in **John 17:20–23**. Why is it good for Christians to have unity with each other? How can you encourage unity in the believers around you?

____

____

____

____

____

____

____

The Sermon on the Mount

Vocabulary

- **The Sermon on the Mount** – The longest message from Jesus recorded in the Gospels

- **The Beatitudes** – Eight "blessings" that begin Jesus' Sermon on the Mount

- **Blessed** – Having special favor, grace, or happiness

- **Peacemaker** – A person who ends conflict in a lasting way

- **Hallowed** – Set apart as special, sacred, or holy

25-A The Beatitudes

In Matthew 5–7 and Luke 6:17–49, you can read the "Sermon on the Mount." This sermon includes some of Jesus' most important teachings. Here Jesus explained how citizens of God's kingdom should think and act.

► Read **Luke 6:17–19**. Before Jesus spoke to His disciples, what did He do for the crowds?

____

____

► Read the eight Beatitudes in **Matthew 5:1–12**. In the following table, record who is **blessed** and how God blesses them. The first is given for you.

Blessed are . . .		Because . . .
Verse 3 – **The poor in spirit**	They depend entirely on God.	The **kingdom of heaven** is theirs.
Verse 4 – _______________	They grieve over sin and how it hurts people.	They will be _______________

Blessed are . . .		Because . . .
Verse 5 – _______________ _______________	They submit to others and to God.	They will inherit _______________.
Verse 6 – _______________ _______________ _______________	They long to live as God commands.	They will be _______________.
Verse 7 – _______________ _______________	They show compassion to others.	They will receive _______________.
Verse 8 – _______________ _______________	They are wholeheartedly dedicated to God.	They will _______________ God.
Verse 9 – _______________ _______________	They help others resolve conflict and find peace.	They will be called _______________ of God.
Verse 10 – _______________ _______________ _______________	They suffer hardship for following God.	The _______________ _______________ is theirs.

These are all Christ-like attitudes that appear in believers who follow God. Christians will show love and mercy to others. Christians will even be willing to suffer, mourn, and be persecuted for the sake of Jesus.

We cannot force ourselves to have these attitudes. In our own power, we cannot overcome our natural tendency to sin. But over time, as we meditate on Christ through His Word, the Spirit will grow us. We will see these attitudes and these blessings.

▶ Look again at the beatitudes and answer the following questions.

⊙ Which attitude do you need the most help with?

____

⊙ Which of these promised blessings gives you the most hope?

____

____

25-B Love and the Law

Jesus taught many lessons in His sermon, but He also needed to *un-teach* some things. For years, the Pharisees and other religious leaders had twisted the way people understood the Old Testament Law. The Pharisees added their own rules and ignored the purpose behind God's commands.

So Jesus explained that we should do more than just follow rules. We should also love people like God does.

▶ Read **Matthew 5:21–24** and answer the following questions.

- Which of the Ten Commandments did Jesus mention here? (v. 21)

____

- Who will also face God's judgment? (v. 22)

____

____

____

Anger is not a sin by itself, but we do wrong when we nurture that anger and let it hurt other people. Our uncontrolled anger might not actually murder someone, but we can still tear people down with our words.

- If we go to worship God and realize that we've wronged someone, what should we do? (v. 24)

____

____

▶ Read **Matthew 5:38–42** again. What attitudes or character traits would someone need to have in order to obey this command?

____

____

____

▶ Read **Matthew 5:43–48** and answer the following questions.

- What is easy to do? (vv. 43, 46–47)

____

____

- But when we show love to our enemies, who are we acting like? (vv. 45, 48)

____

25-C Prayer and Forgiveness

Many Christians think of prayer like a speech or a magic formula. They believe their prayers will impress people or convince God to give them something.

▶ But in **Matthew 6:9–13**, Jesus gave His disciples an example of a good prayer. Write the entire prayer below.

____

____

____

____

____

____

____

____

____

⊙ In the text above, **draw a rectangle** around the phrase that refers to our physical needs.

⊙ **Draw a star** near the word that calls God "holy" or "sacred." Note the vocabulary on page 118.

⊙ **Draw a circle** around any phrases that show a desire to obey God.

▶ Note what Jesus said afterward in **Matthew 6:14–15**. What is one good reason to forgive others?

____

____

► Read **Matthew 7:1–5** and mark the best answer to each question below.

⊙ **What do you think Jesus meant when He said not to "judge"? (vv. 1–2)**

- [ ] Don't try to understand the difference between good and evil.
- [ ] Don't condemn people as worthless—or they may attack you with your own words.
- [ ] Never tell someone that they've done something wrong.
- [ ] Never become a judge for a court.

⊙ **By talking about pieces of wood in your eye, what principle did Jesus teach? (vv. 3–5)**

- [ ] Everyone in Israel kept running head first into trees.
- [ ] You can't help people avoid sin if you've ever sinned yourself.
- [ ] Small sins don't matter.
- [ ] You can't help people correct small sins when you keep committing even bigger sins.

Winning Your Race

► Read **Matthew 7:12**. How did Jesus summarize the rules from the Old Testament Law and Prophets?

____

____

____

► For each of the following situations, mark what you'd like others to do for you.

I keep getting into huge fights with my family.	☐ Others could join my side so my family members will feel terrible. ☐ Others could attack me for ever disagreeing with family members. ☐ Others could help me understand the conflict and make peace.
I don't understand how to do my school work.	☐ Others could give me answers to all the questions. ☐ Others could make fun of me for not understanding the work. ☐ Others could help explain the concepts, as my teacher allows.
I'm sad about something that happened to me.	☐ Others could tell me to stop feeling sad. ☐ Others could show that they care and want to help me keep going. ☐ Others could tell me that everyone will always feel sad forever.
I sinned and hurt someone.	☐ Others should ignore it. It's OK if I keep hurting people. ☐ Others should correct me and show me how to do better next time. ☐ Others should hurt me the same way I hurt them.

The Crucifixion

Vocabulary

- **Crucifixion** – A method of execution; killing someone by attaching them to an upright piece of wood and leaving them to die

- **Foreknowledge** – To know something ahead of time; to know about an event before it happens

- **Scourge / Flog** – To beat or lash with a whip

- **The Council / Sanhedrin** – A group of Jewish leaders who made legal and religious decisions for the people

- **Blasphemy** – Insulting God or something sacred; saying something untrue about God

26-A His Foreknowledge

The Father sent Jesus to die for our sin, so Jesus knew about His death from the very beginning. Jesus also knew how terrible His suffering would be, but He still submitted to the Father's plan. He chose to endure this for our sake.

▶ Nothing about Jesus' crucifixion was a surprise. Read the following passages and complete the summaries.

Matthew 16:21	Jesus tells His disciples that He must go to ________________________, where the religious leaders will hurt Him. He will be ________________ and then raised again on the ________________ day.
Matthew 17:22–23	In Galilee, Jesus again says that the ________________________ will be ________________________ into the hands of men. These people will ________________ Him, but He will rise again on the third day afterward.

<table>
<tr><td>Luke
18:31–34</td><td>A third time, Jesus says that the Son of Man will be delivered over to the _______________________. He will be mocked, mistreated, and _______________ upon. They will ___________________ Him and kill Him, but He will rise again.</td></tr>
</table>

► It was difficult for Jesus to know about this suffering ahead of time. Read **Luke 22:39–44**, which records what Jesus prayed the night before His death. Answer the following questions.

- ◉ What request did Jesus make to the Father? (v. 42)

  ____

  ____

- ◉ What do you think He meant by "this cup"?

  ____

- ◉ What was more important to Jesus? (v. 42)

  ____

- ◉ Jesus is both God and human. How did His body struggle during this time? (v. 44)

  ____

  ____

26-B His Innocence

Like the Passover lamb, Jesus was a perfect and spotless sacrifice. As the only truly innocent person, Jesus suffered the punishment for our sins. God executed perfect justice on Himself.

► The religious leaders who hated Jesus did not understand God's plan. They simply wanted Jesus dead. Read two different accounts of Jesus' arrest in **Matthew 26:47–56** and **Luke 22:47–53**. Then order the events below from **1** to **8**.

	The crowd armed with weapons approached Jesus to seize Him.
	All of Jesus' disciples left Him and fled.
	Jesus told His disciples not to fight. He did not need their protection.
	One of the disciples struck a servant of the High Priest and cut off his ear.
	Jesus healed the ear of the servant.
	Jesus' disciples asked Him if they should fight back with their swords.
	Judas found Jesus and greeted Him with a kiss.
	Jesus asked the crowds and the religious leaders why they arrested Him at night.

► Before His death, Jesus was judged by several different authorities. Read the passages below and explain how Jesus answered those who accused Him.

Passage	Judges	How did Jesus answer His accusers?
John 18:19–24	Annas	**Verses 20, 23** – He said that He did not teach anything in ________________. He told them to say what He did wrong.
Matthew 26:59–68	Caiaphas and the *Sanhedrin*, or *Council*	**Verses 63-64** – He said that yes, He was the ______________ ________________________________.
Luke 23:1–5	Pilate, the Roman governor	**Verse 3** – He said that yes, He was the ______________ ________________________________.
Luke 23:6–11	Herod, the Jewish king	**Verse 9** – To Herod's questions, Jesus ______________ ________________________________.

26-C His Suffering

Pilate told the people that he could find nothing wrong with Jesus—certainly nothing to deserve death. But the religious leaders stirred up the people to demand Jesus' death.

► Read **Matthew 27:15–31** and answer the following:

◉ Instead of Jesus, what murderous rebel did the people demand that Pilate release? (v. 21)

____

◉ What did Pilate do to Jesus before handing Him over to be crucified? (v. 26)

____

◉ How did the Roman soldiers mock Jesus? (vv. 27–30)

____

____

____

____

____

____

____

► Continue reading in **Matthew 27:33–50** and mark the correct ending to each sentence.

Verse 33: Jesus was crucified at the "place of the skull"—also known as . . .

| ☐ Golgotha. | ☐ Jerusalem. | ☐ Judea. |

Verse 34: After tasting it, Jesus refused to drink the sour wine mixed with . . .

| ☐ spices. | ☐ gall, a bitter liquid. | ☐ clear water. |

Verse 35: The soldiers gambled over who would get Jesus' . . .

| ☐ land. | ☐ money. | ☐ clothing. |

Verse 37: They placed a sign above Jesus' head to show His crime. It said . . .

| ☐ "This is Jesus, a Blasphemer of God." | ☐ "This is Jesus, the Messiah of Humanity." | ☐ "This is Jesus, the King of the Jews." |

Verses 39–44: Almost everyone around mocked Jesus and said He could not . . .

| ☐ save Himself. | ☐ raise Himself. | ☐ avenge Himself. |

Verse 45: Beginning at noon and lasting for three hours, there was . . .

- ☐ fog, rain, and hail.
- ☐ darkness over the land.
- ☐ lightning in the clouds.

Verse 46: Jesus cried out and asked why God had . . .

- ☐ forsaken Him.
- ☐ mocked Him.
- ☐ killed Him.

Verse 50: After Jesus cried out again, He . . .

- ☐ wept.
- ☐ prayed.
- ☐ died.

Winning Your Race

It's impossible to understand how the Trinity works, but Jesus, the Spirit, and the Father are all One. God is perfectly unified, so the Son submitted to the Father's plan. Jesus endured the pain and mockery to save us.

► We will not face anything as difficult as what Jesus did, but we can have trouble submitting to God's will. Think about the following statements and mark how often they apply to you.

	Rarely		Sometimes		Often
I show respect for others by treating them the way I would want to be treated.	1	2	3	4	5
I give thanks despite what happens in my life.	1	2	3	4	5
I talk to God about my hopes and my fears.	1	2	3	4	5
I trust God to take care of my needs and bless me in ways He thinks best.	1	2	3	4	5
I study the Bible to learn more about God.	1	2	3	4	5
I spend time with other Christians, encouraging them and sharing my own struggles.	1	2	3	4	5
I serve others by doing good and helping people in need.	1	2	3	4	5
I tell others what Jesus has done for me.	1	2	3	4	5

The Resurrection

Vocabulary

- **Resurrection** – The event in which someone dead becomes alive again

- **Apostle** – A "sent one"; a witness of the resurrection of Jesus

- **Ascension** – The event in which one rises upward; in Scripture, Jesus' rise from Earth to heaven

- **The Great Commission** – The task Jesus gave His followers to make more disciples for Him

27-A Jesus Lives Again

After Jesus died, His followers must have felt crushed and alone. But hope was not lost. Just as Jesus had foretold His death, He had also prophesied His resurrection.

▶ Read the two accounts in **Matthew 28:1–10** and **Luke 24:1–12**, and then answer the following:

⊙ On the third day after Jesus' death, who visited His tomb first?

____

____

⊙ Did they expect to find the tomb empty? ☐ Yes ☐ No

Explain your answer. ____________________________

____

⊙ What happened just before they arrived?

____

____

⊙ What did the angel say had happened?

____

⊙ How did the women feel after hearing this news?

____

- ◉ As some of the women were leaving, who appeared to them? _______________________

- ◉ What were the women told to do?

  ____

  ____

  ____

- ◉ At first, did most of the disciples believe these women? ☐ Yes ☐ No

▶ Read **John 20:1–18**, which focuses on what Mary Magdalene saw. Answer the following:

- ◉ What did Mary do immediately after seeing the empty tomb?

  ____

- ◉ After the two disciples saw the empty tomb, what message did Jesus entrust to Mary?

  ____

  ____

27-B Jesus Appears to His Followers

For forty days after His resurrection, Jesus appeared to many of His followers and spent time with them. He spent time convincing them that He was truly alive. He loved and cared for His disciples. He would not leave them scared or unprepared for the days ahead.

▶ Imagine you were one of Jesus' disciples at this time. What would it take to convince you that He was alive again?

  ____

  ____

  ____

▶ Read the following passages and match them to the people described.

Luke 24:13–18 – We were traveling to Emmaus when Jesus appeared to us. At first, we did not recognize Him.	**A.**	Some of the disciples
John 20:11–18 – When Jesus first appeared to me, I thought He was a gardener.	**B.**	Mary
John 20:19–23 – We were hiding behind locked doors when Jesus appeared and showed us His hands and side.	**C.**	Thomas
John 20:24–29 – I would not believe Jesus was alive until I could see and feel His wounds for myself.	**D.**	Cleopas and his companion
John 21:1–13 – Jesus appeared to me and six other disciples, and we all shared a breakfast of fish.	**E.**	Simon Peter

► In one of his letters to Corinth, Paul explained why Jesus' resurrection is so important to our faith. Read **1 Corinthians 15:3–8** and list some of the people who saw Jesus after He rose again.

Verse 5	______________________________, also called Simon Peter
Verse 5	The ______________________________
Verse 6	Over ______________________________ believers at one time
Verse 7	______________________________, Jesus' brother
Verse 7	All the ______________________________
Verse 8	Finally, to ______________________________

► Continue reading in **1 Corinthians 15:14–19**. Write one reason why Christ's resurrection is so important to Christian beliefs.

____

____

____

27-C Jesus Ascends into Heaven

► Before Jesus' *ascension* into heaven, He gave a final message to His disciples. Read what He said in **Matthew 28:16–20** and answer the following questions.

⊙ Where did Jesus meet with the eleven disciples?

____

⊙ Jesus wanted to encourage the disciples. What did He say He had? (v. 18)

____

⊙ Jesus gave His followers the **Great Commission**. List what He told them to do. (vv. 19–20)

1. Go and ____ . . .

2. ______________________________ them in the ______________________ of the Father, the Son, and the Holy Spirit . . .

3. ______________________________ them to ______________________________ everything that Jesus had commanded.

⊙ Finally, what did Jesus promise? (v. 20)

____

____

▶ Read another account of the ascension in **Acts 1:3–11** and complete the summaries.

Verse 3	Over _______________ days, Jesus appeared to His disciples and spoke about the _______________________ of God.
Verses 4–5	Jesus told them to wait in _______________________________. They would soon be baptized—not with water, but with the _______________________________.
Verse 8	The disciples would be _______________________ for Jesus all over the world.
Verses 9–11	After Jesus ascended, two men in white asked the disciples why they were staring into _______________________. Jesus would return some day in the same way that He left.

Winning Your Race

▶ If we trust that our Savior has risen, we can live a courageous new life with Him. Read the command in **Colossians 3:1–4** and explain how you might follow it.

____

____

____

____

____

The Power of the Spirit

Vocabulary

- **Pentecost** – The "fiftieth day" after Easter; when the Spirit first arrived to bless the Church

- **Tongues** – In the New Testament, a term for different languages

28-A God Sends His Spirit

▶ Remember when Jesus promised the Holy Spirit? Look back at **John 14:26** and answer the following questions.

◉ What name does Jesus use for the One sent by the Father?

____

◉ What two important things would the Holy Spirit do?

1. _______________________________________

2. _______________________________________

▶ Read ahead in **John 15:18–27** and answer the following questions.

◉ What did Jesus warn His disciples about? (vv. 18–21)

____

____

◉ Can people know about Jesus and still hate Him? (vv. 24–25) ☐ Yes ☐ No

◉ But God would not leave believers alone in this world. What two names does Jesus call the Holy Spirit? (v. 26)

____

◉ What would the Spirit do through Jesus' disciples? (vv. 26–27)

____

► God fulfilled His promise at **Pentecost**, the "fiftieth day" after the resurrection of Jesus. Read what happened in **Acts 2:1–12**.

  ◉ Draw a picture of the miracle described in **verses 1–4**.

  ◉ What special ability did the Holy Spirit give to these believers? (vv. 4–8)

  ____

  ____

  ◉ What did the believers use this ability to do? (v. 11)

  ____

  ____

  ◉ Why do you think God gave this gift to the early Church? How could it help?

  ____

  ____

  ____

28-B Peter's Transformation

► While Jesus still served on Earth, Simon Peter was a passionate, outspoken follower. Read the following passages and match each sentence to its correct ending.

	Matthew 4:18–20 – When Jesus called him, Peter . . .	**A.** called Him the Christ (Messiah), the Son of God.
	Matthew 14:22–33 – When Jesus walked on water to reach the disciples' boat, Peter . . .	**B.** immediately left his fishing nets.
	Matthew 16:13–17 – When Jesus asked His disciples who people thought He was, Peter . . .	**C.** rebuked Him.
	Matthew 16:21–22 – When Jesus explained that He would one day need to die, Peter . . .	**D.** denied Him three times.
	Matthew 26:69–75 – While Jesus was on trial, Peter . . .	**E.** asked to walk out and meet Him.

Peter's courage failed whenever he took his eyes off Christ. Peter could not be the hero of his own story. He needed to depend on God for his strength.

After the resurrection, Jesus charged Peter with caring for the people of the Church. Though Peter was far from perfect, he threw himself into this task. He just had no idea how big this Church would become.

▶ Read the following verses from **Acts 2** and answer the questions.

⊙ **Verse 14** – Right after the arrival of the Holy Spirit, what did Peter do?

____

⊙ **Verses 16–18** – Who had prophesied about the work of God's Spirit?

____

⊙ **Verses 36–38** – What was Peter's main message?

____

____

____

⊙ **Verse 41** – How many people believed what he said? _______________________________

▶ Read **Acts 4:1–4**. Even after Peter was arrested, how many believed? ____________________

The religious leaders in Jerusalem were not happy. They thought they had put an end to Jesus, but now He had more disciples than ever. The leaders released Peter in the hope that he would eventually quiet down.

28-C The Spirit in All Believers

▶ The Spirit was not finished teaching Peter. Read **Acts 10** and fill in the following blanks.

In the city of Caesarea, there was a man named ___________________________ who

served as a ___________________________ in the Roman army. He saw an angel of God

who told him to send for _________________________ in Joppa.

The next day, while the messengers were still traveling, Peter went up on the

_______________________ to pray. He happened to be hungry, and he saw a vision of a

giant ___________________ coming down from the sky. Inside were all kinds of animals.

A voice told Peter to rise up, _______________, and _______________. Peter refused,

saying that he had never eaten anything ___________________________ or unclean. The

voice told him not to call "___________________________" anything that God had made

clean.

This conversation repeated twice more before the vision ended. While Peter wondered what it meant, the messengers arrived for him. The _________________ told him to go with them, and they all left together the next day.

When they arrived in Caesarea, Cornelius had gathered his _____________________ and close _________________. Cornelius _____________________ at Peter's feet to worship him, but Peter said that he too was just a ______________.

Peter told everyone gathered that it was unlawful for him, as a ______________, to spend time so close with people from another nation. But God had shown him that he should not call anyone _______________________ or unclean.

After Cornelius explained the vision he had seen, Peter began to share the gospel. He said that God accepts people from every _________________, so long as they fear Him and do right. He explained how Jesus had preached and healed—how He had died and then rose again on the _________________ day. Not everyone saw the risen Christ, but many witnesses did, including those who ______________ and _________________ with Him after He rose from the dead. Jesus is the judge of the living and the dead, and everyone who _____________________ in Him receives forgiveness.

While Peter was still talking, the _______________________ fell on everyone who heard his words. The Jewish believers with Peter were amazed that this had happened to _________________. Cornelius' family and friends showed the same signs as the believers at Pentecost, so Peter had them _______________________ in Jesus' name.

After spending time with these new believers, Peter returned to Jerusalem, telling the church everything that had happened. The Jewish believers rejoiced that God had also offered His grace to the Gentiles.

► In your own words, describe the lesson that God taught Peter.

____

____

____

____

____

Winning Your Race

► Complete the following form as best as you can.

<table>
<tr><td>Name:</td><td>☐ Male ☐ Female</td></tr>
<tr><td colspan="2">Place of Birth:</td></tr>
<tr><td colspan="2">In what country or countries do you have citizenship?</td></tr>
<tr><td colspan="2">How old are you?
☐ 6–10 yrs. ☐ 11–15 yrs. ☐ 16–25 yrs. ☐ 26–40 yrs. ☐ 41–60 yrs. ☐ 60+ yrs.</td></tr>
<tr><td colspan="2">Do you think of your family as . . .
☐ very poor ☐ somewhat poor ☐ neither poor nor rich ☐ somewhat rich ☐ very rich</td></tr>
</table>

► Read what Paul wrote in **1 Corinthians 12:12–14** again, along with **Galatlans 3:27–28** and **James 2:1–9**. How does the information above affect God's love for you?

____

____

► If God's Spirit can save and work through anyone, how should you treat others in His Church?

____

____

____

____

____

____

Revealing the Future

Vocabulary

- **Sovereignty** – Power and authority; in Scripture, God's sole rulership over everything

- **Alpha and Omega** – The first and last letters of the Greek alphabet; in the Book of Revelation, a phrase referring to God's power over all things, beginning to end

- **Justify** – To declare that someone is innocent or righteous; to defend something as right

29-A God's Sovereignty

Decades after the resurrection of Jesus, the last of the twelve disciples was living his final years in exile on an island called Patmos. During this time, the apostle received a vision, which he recorded in a letter now called the Book of Revelation.

▶ Read **Revelation 1:1–11** and answer the following questions.

⊙ Which apostle received this revelation from Jesus? (v. 1) _______________________________

⊙ What does this revelation show? (v. 1)

____

⊙ Where was this letter sent? (v. 4)

____

⊙ What did John want his readers to remember? (v. 7)

____

____

⊙ How does God describe Himself to John? (v. 8)

  ▪ He is the _____________________ and _____________________.

  ▪ He is, He _____________, and He _____________________.

  ▪ He is the _____________________.

○ John was exiled to Patmos for preaching the gospel. One Sunday, he heard a voice as loud as a trumpet. What did the voice tell him to do? (vv. 9–11)

____

____

Christians cannot understand everything described in the Book of Revelation, but we can trust its main message. God is in complete control. No matter what happens on Earth or in heaven, He has a plan to set everything right, and no one can stop Him.

▶ Read the following passages and complete the summaries.

Psalm 135:6	The Lord does whatever He _____________________ in heaven, on the earth, in the seas, and in every deep place.
Psalm 147:5	God is powerful. His understanding _____________________.
Isaiah 46:9–10	He alone is God. There is _____________________ like Him.
Isaiah 55:11	God's word will not return to Him _____________________, nor will His word fail to accomplish His purpose.
Daniel 4:35	No one can hold back God's hand or say, "_____________________ _____________________ "

29-B Prophecy in the Bible

We can only know the present and remember the past, but time does not limit God. He has always been and always will be. He is above time, so He knows our past, present, and future all at once. Nothing can catch Him by surprise.

▶ Just as important—God fulfills all His promises. Read the following prophecies and fill in the blanks. Then match each prophecy to its fulfillment on the next page.

A. Genesis 15:3–4	Abraham's own biological son would be his _____________.
B. Exodus 3:7–8	God would give Israel a _____________ that was good, large, and flowing with milk and honey.
C. Isaiah 53:10–11	God's righteous _____________ would **justify** many people and bear their iniquities.
D. Jeremiah 30:3	The Lord would bring His people back to the _____________.
E. Mark 8:31	After suffering through rejection and death, Jesus would rise again.

Prophecy	Fulfillment
	Genesis 21:1–3 – Sarah conceived and gave birth to Isaac.
	Joshua 24:11–14 – God protected His people from enemy armies. He gave the Israelites land and cities they did not earn for themselves.
	Ezra 1:1–4 – Cyrus, the king of Persia, proclaimed that the Jewish exiles could return to Jerusalem to build a temple to God.
	Matthew 28:6 – The angel said that the tomb was empty.
	Romans 3:23–25 – God justified us by His grace through the death of Jesus.

Often, prophecies in Scripture do not come to pass right away. And sometimes, a prophecy might have *two* fulfillments—one in the near future and then a greater fulfillment in the far future.

► It can be difficult to wait on God to fulfill His promises. Some of the early Christians faced this kind of test. Read **2 Peter 3:3–9** and mark the following statements as true or false. Write the numbers of the verses that helped you decide. For each false statement, rewrite it correctly.

People will deny God's promise because the world has kept changing since the beginning of creation.	☐ True ☐ False	Verse:

Correction: ____

____

God holds the world together with His word until the day of judgment.	☐ True ☐ False	Verse:

Correction: ____

____

A thousand of our years is like a thousand years to God.	☐ True ☐ False	Verse:

Correction: ____

____

God is patient in fulfilling promises because He wants to punish more people.	☐ True ☐ False	Verse:

Correction: ____

____

29-C The Beginning and the End

God created a perfect world, but humanity fell into sin. Jesus Christ gave us a path back to God, but His plan is not yet complete. In the Book of Revelation, John describes how Christ will right every wrong.

▶ Read the following passages in **Revelation** and complete the summaries.

Since the Beginning	In the End
Satan was free to tempt people (1 Pet. 5:8)	**20:10** – The devil was thrown into the ______________________ __________________________________, to be tormented forever.
God created the heavens and the earth (Gen. 1:1).	**21:1** – John saw a ______________ heaven and earth. The old ones ____________________________________.
God banished humanity from His garden (Gen. 3:22–24).	**21:3** – God will ___________________ with His people.
Sin brought pain, suffering, and death (Gen. 3:16–19).	**21:4** – God will wipe away _____________________________ from their eyes. There will be no death, sadness, or pain.
Israel betrayed God like an unfaithful wife (Jer. 3:20).	**21:9–10** – An angel showed the Lamb's ___________________, which was the new Jerusalem coming down from heaven.
Israel worshiped God in the Temple, but it was destroyed (Ezra 5:12).	**21:22–24** – John saw no ____________________ in the new city, nor did it need a _____________ or ________________ to shine—all because God was there.
Sin passed on to all people (Rom. 5:12).	**21:27** – No sinful person will ______________________ the city.

Winning Your Race

▶ God promises to give His children a new world. Complete the table below.

Three Things You Don't Expect to See in Heaven	Three Things You Do Expect to See in Heaven
__________________________________	__________________________________
__________________________________	__________________________________
__________________________________	__________________________________

Messages from the Son

Vocabulary

- **Tribulation** – Great suffering, hardship, or trouble

30-A A Vision of Christ

John wrote the Book of Revelation around the year AD 90. This was about sixty years after the resurrection and ascension of Jesus. By this time, many of the original disciples had passed away. But in the early church, there was an interesting rumor about John.

▶ Read the end of John's Gospel in **John 21:20–25** and answer the following questions.

◉ John didn't often write his own name, so he called himself the "disciple whom Jesus loved." What false rumor spread about John? (v. 23)

____

____

◉ What did Jesus really ask Peter?

____

____

____

▶ Like everyone else from that time, John died before the return of Jesus. But in John's final days, he did see Jesus again—just not like he remembered. Read **Revelation 1:10–18** and complete the following:

Verse 12	Turning around, John saw seven golden _______________________________.
Verse 13	In the middle was one like ___________________________, clothed in a long robe and a golden _______________ around His chest.

Verse 14	His hair was the color __________________ like wool and __________________, and His eyes were like _______________________________________.
Verse 15	His feet were like _______________________________________ in a furnace, and His voice was like the sound of _______________________________________.
Verse 16	He held seven __________________ in His right hand. Out of His mouth came a sharp _______________________________________. His face was like the __________________ shining.

⊙ How did John react to seeing this Person? (v. 17)

____

⊙ What did this Person say to encourage John? (v. 17)

____

► Note how this "Son of Man" described Himself in **verses 17–18**. How could John know that this Person was Jesus?

____

____

____

30-B The Seven Churches

► Read **Revelation 1:19–20** and fill in the blanks below. In John's vision . . .

⊙ The seven stars represented the __________________________ of the seven churches.

⊙ The seven _______________________________________ represented the seven churches.

► The seven churches were located in seven cities across Asia. Jesus gave John messages to pass on to each of them. Read the following passages in **Revelation** and complete the summaries.

Church	Encouragement	Challenge
1. **Ephesus**	**2:2** – Jesus saw their hard work and knew they did not tolerate evil people in the church. They tested people who claimed to be _______________________.	**2:4–5** – They left _______________ _______________________________. They needed to repent.

Church	Encouragement	Challenge
2. **Smyrna**	**2:9** – They endured *tribulation*, including poverty, hurtful lies, and imprisonment.	**2:10** – If they were faithful even to death, Jesus would give them __________________________ __________________________.
3. **Pergamum**	**2:13** – They __________________ __________________________ to Christ's name. They did not deny their faith in Him.	**2:14** – They encouraged others to sin by eating food sacrificed to _______________ and by committing __________________ __________________. They needed to repent.
4. **Thyatira**	**2:19** – Jesus knew all about their __________________, their love, their faith, their service, and their __________________________. They kept doing better.	**2:20, 24–25** – They allowed a false __________________________ to lead others into sin. God would judge her, but the others in the city should repent and stay faithful.
5. **Sardis**	**3:4** – Some of them had not yet " __________________ their __________________________."	**3:2** – They needed to stay alert and __________________________ the things that remained. Their work wasn't yet complete.
6. **Philadelphia**	**3:8** – Despite their weakness, they kept Jesus' _______________ and did not deny His _______________.	**3:11** – To keep their crown, they needed to __________________ to what they already had.
7. **Laodicea**	**3:15–17** – They weren't cold or hot, but __________________________. They were physically rich but spiritually starving.	**3:18–19** – They needed gold from Christ that had been refined in _______________. They needed spiritual riches that came through correction and discipline.

30-C The Early Church

The seven churches in Revelation were not the only ones during this time. Christian assemblies first began in Jerusalem but quickly spread around the Mediterranean. By the end of John's life, believers had reached North Africa, Europe, and maybe even India. In the centuries afterward, the gospel would reach every part of the globe.

► Some of the seven churches from Revelation are labeled in the map below. Label the four missing churches by using their **orange numbers** from pages 142–143.

► Read the following passages and complete the summaries. Then label the locations by using the matching **purple letters** on the map.

Acts 1:4	Jesus told the disciples to wait in ______________________ (**A**) until the Holy Spirit arrived.
Acts 10:1	The centurion Cornelius, who lived in ______________________ (**B**), was one of the first Gentiles to accept Christ.
Acts 11:26	It was in the city of ______________________ (**C**) that followers of Jesus first became known as "Christians."

Acts **16:11–12**	On Paul's second missionary journey, he went to ________________________ (**D**). Here Paul and Silas survived an earthquake while they were in prison.
Acts **18:1–3**	Paul met his fellow workers Aquila and Priscilla in ________________________ (**E**). He wrote at least two long letters to the believers here.
Acts **23:11**	God told Paul to testify about Christ in ________________________ (**F**). Paul came to this city as a prisoner, but he shared the gospel in Caesar's house.
Revelation **1:9**	John was exiled to the island of ________________________ (**G**) for the sake of the gospel.

Winning Your Race

▶ If Jesus described you like He did the seven churches, what do you think He would say?

You endure difficulties. ☐	☐	You give up during difficulties.
You become close friends with wise people. ☐	☐	You become close friends with evil people.
You hold fast to Jesus' name. ☐	☐	You deny being with Jesus.
You show love and kindness to others. ☐	☐	You live to serve yourself.
You examine what people say about God. ☐	☐	You accept whatever you hear about God.
You repent when you realize your sin. ☐	☐	You allow your sin to continue.
You serve God's kingdom wholeheartedly. ☐	☐	You are apathetic toward God's kingdom.

The Church in Heaven

<table>
<tr><th>Vocabulary</th></tr>
<tr><td>• Archangel – An angel appointed over a special task; a chief angel</td></tr>
<tr><td>• Rapture – To grab or take away; a name for the event in which Christ takes believers to be with Him in heaven</td></tr>
<tr><td>• Saint – A sacred or holy person; in Scripture, a term for a believer or Christian</td></tr>
</table>

31-A The Resurrection of the Dead

John was not the only apostle who wrote about the future. We can also find prophecies in the letters of Paul.

▶ The believers in Thessalonica knew that Christ would return one day, but they wondered what would happen to believers who had already died. Would Jesus remember all His followers? Read how Paul responded in **1 Thessalonians 4:13–18** and order the events from **1** to **4**.

	Christians who are alive will join Christ and the others in the sky.
	The Lord will descend from heaven, marked by a shout, the voice of an ***archangel***, and the trumpet of God.
	The Church will remain forever with the Lord in heaven.
	Christians who are dead will rise back to life.

Many Christians call this event the ***rapture***. After this moment, Christians will finally be with Jesus, with nothing separating us. We will have perfect fellowship with Him and with each other.

▶ Read more about this event in **1 Corinthians 15:50–53** and answer the following questions.

◉ What cannot inherit God's kingdom? (v. 50)

____

- Paul explains that not all believers will "sleep," or die, before Christ's return. But what *will* happen to all of us? (v. 51)

  ____

- How quickly will this happen? (v. 52)

  ____

- When the trumpet sounds, what will Christ transform all believers into? (vv. 52–53)

  ____

▶ Read **Philippians 3:20–21**. In heaven, who will we become like? _______________________

▶ Finally, read **Titus 2:11–14**. If we believe that Christ will come back for us one day, what should we do? Use your own words to summarize what Paul encouraged Titus to do.

- **Verse 12—**____

  ____

  ____

  ____

- **Verse 13—**____

  ____

  ____

31-B The Judgment Seat of Christ

When Jesus died on the cross, He endured all the punishment for our sin. If we have trusted in Him, we will not be judged for that sin again. But when believers stand before God in heaven, He will tell us how we honored Him or dishonored Him with our lives.

▶ Read **2 Corinthians 5:1–10** and answer the following questions.

- What do you think Paul means when he writes about our earthly "house" or "tent"? (vv. 1–4)

  ____

  ____

- What is God preparing us for? (vv. 4–5)

  ____

  ____

- While we're here on Earth and can't see Jesus face to face, how must we walk? (vv. 6–7)

  ____

◉ What is our goal? (v. 9)

____

◉ What will happen when we appear before Christ for judgment? (v. 10)

____

____

____

▶ God saves believers by His grace, and we should respond by teaching others about Him. Read what Paul wrote in **1 Corinthians 3:9–15** and complete the summaries below.

Verse 9	Believers work with God. We are like His farm field or _____________________.
Verse 10	God gave Paul grace to lay down a _____________________, which other people could build upon carefully.
Verse 11	_____________________ is the only foundation that people can use.
Verse 12	People can build on this foundation with materials like _____________ _____________ _____________ _____________ _____________ . . .
Verse 13	. . . But their work will be tested by _____________ to reveal its quality.
Verse 14	If someone's work survives, that person will receive a _____________________.
Verse 15	If the work is burned up, the person will still be _____________________, but the work will be lost.

Our teaching and good works will only last if they honor God and stay true to Him. We should lead only by encouraging others to follow God. If we instead try to gain popularity for ourselves, our work will not survive God's judgment. We should not waste our effort.

31-C The Lamb and the Throne

When John caught a glimpse of the future, many of His visions showed God's throne room in heaven. The apostle saw fantastic things that he could barely describe. God's glory overwhelmed him.

▶ Read the description in **Revelation 4:1–7** and sketch a rough diagram of what John saw around the throne. Label whatever items you can.

Throne of God

▶ Read **Revelation 5:1–10** and mark the best ending to the following sentences.

In God's right hand, John saw a scroll bound with seven . . .

☐ golden locks.	☐ words.	☐ seals.

An angel asked who was . . .

☐ wise enough to re-write the scroll.	☐ worthy enough to open the scroll.	☐ strong enough to destroy the scroll.

At first, it seemed like no one could open or read the scroll, so John . . .

☐ opened it himself.	☐ thought the scroll must be unimportant.	☐ began to weep.

An elder in heaven told John that the scroll could be opened by . . .

☐ the Lion of the tribe of Judah, the Root of David.	☐ the Great Shepherd, the Door to Eternal Life.	☐ the Promised Messiah, the branch of Jesse.

► How else did John describe the Church? Read the following passages and fill in the blanks.

Revelation 7:9–10	A great _______________________ from all nations, tribes, peoples, and languages, praising God the Father and the Lamb
Revelation 19:6	A crowd with a voice like _______________________ and thunder, all praising God and rejoicing in Him

Winning Your Race

► Think about the believers in John's day. They were persecuted on all sides by people who hated Jesus. The Romans had destroyed Jerusalem, and Christians had little power or influence. Like many Christians throughout history, they had good reason to be discouraged. How can the passages about God's throne room encourage us?

____

____

____

____

Judging the World

Vocabulary

- **The Day of the Lord** – In Scripture, a time when God fulfills His promises in an undeniable way

- **The Elect** – In Scripture, another term for Christians; people chosen by God

- **Famine** – A time when many people have very little food

- **Martyr** – Someone killed for their religious beliefs

- **Censer** – A bowl or container for burning incense

- **Wormwood** – A very bitter herb

- **Antichrist** – Someone who is against Jesus Christ

32-A The Day of the Lord

In Scripture, we can find many references to the Day of the Lord. Some of these refer to the events of Revelation, and some refer to things that have already happened. In every case, the Day of the Lord marks the time when God enforces His justice in the world.

▶ Read the following passages and answer the questions.

◉ **Isaiah 13:6, 11** – In the Day described by Isaiah, what would God do?

____

____

◉ **Ezekiel 30:3–4** – In the Day described by Ezekiel, what would happen to the nations?

____

____

◉ **Joel 2:11** – What does the Day of the Lord reveal about God?

____

- **Obadiah 1:15** – In the Day described by Obadiah, how will the wicked be punished?

____

____

- **Malachi 4:5–6** – What does God promise to do before this Day?

____

____

- **1 Thessalonians 5:2–3** – How will the Day described by Paul arrive?

____

____

- **2 Peter 3:10** – In this Day, what will happen to all the works done in this world?

____

____

► Jesus also prophesied about a Day of the Lord. Read the following verses from **Matthew 24** and match each sentence to its best ending.

	Verse 5 – People will come in Christ's name . . .	**A.** the days of tribulation will be shortened.
	Verse 12 – As sin grows uncontrollably . . .	**B.** will be saved.
	Verse 13 – The one who endures to the end . . .	**C.** and deceive many people by claiming to be Jesus.
	Verse 14 – The gospel will be preached through the entire world . . .	**D.** and then the end will come.
	Verses 21–22 – For the sake of the **elect** . . .	**E.** many people's love will grow cold.
	Verse 35 – Heaven and earth will pass away . . .	**F.** but Jesus' words will not.

God is very merciful. He has told people to repent and warned them about His future judgment on sin. He sent His Son to rescue people in sin. He wants people to repent of their sin and come to Him rather than suffer this judgment (2 Pet. 3:9).

► Finally, note **Matthew 24:36**. What should you do if a teacher claims to know when the end times will come?

____

____

____

____

32-B The Tribulation

Beginning in Revelation 6, John describes a time of great trouble and suffering. This is a period of seven years called the Tribulation. During this time, God will punish the world for its sin. This will be one last chance for unbelievers left in the world to see their wickedness and repent.

The Seven Seals

During the Tribulation, God judges the world in three phases. The first set of judgments are represented by seven seals. God commands these seals to be opened one by one.

► Read the following passages and use the words below to fill in the blanks.

angel	black	conquer	Death
famine	hid	Lamb	*martyrs*
red	silence	wars	white

The First Seal **Revelation 6:1–2**	One on a _____________ horse rode out to _____________________.
The Second Seal **Revelation 6:3–4**	A second horseman on a __________ horse began _____________ by removing peace from the world.
The Third Seal **Revelation 6:5–6**	The third horseman on a _________________ horse brought _________________. Wheat and barley became very expensive.
The Fourth Seal **Revelation 6:7–8**	The fourth horseman was named _______________. He rode a horse as pale as ash, and he killed a fourth of the world with many disasters.
The Fifth Seal **Revelation 6:9–11**	When the fifth seal was opened, _________________ for God asked how long before He would judge their killers.
The Sixth Seal **Revelation 6:12–17**	The earth shook while things fell from the sky. People __________ themselves from the wrath of the _________________.
The Seventh Seal **Revelation 8:1–5**	There was _________________ in heaven for half an hour. An _________________ filled a *censer* with fire from God's altar and then threw it to the earth, causing lightning and an earthquake.

The Seven Trumpets

► After the seals are opened, seven angels begin to blow seven trumpets. Just like before, read the following passages and use the words to fill in the blanks.

200,000,000	Ark of the Covenant	bitter	blood
darkened	hail	kingdom	locusts
mountain	scorpions	sun	*Wormwood*

The First Trumpet **Revelation 8:7**	_______________ and fire mixed with blood rained down. A third of the earth, trees, and grass were burned up.
The Second Trumpet **Revelation 8:8–9**	Something like a great, fiery _______________________ was thrown into the sea. A third of the sea became _______________, a third of the sea creatures died, and a third of the ships were destroyed.
The Third Trumpet **Revelation 8:10–11**	A burning star named _______________ fell and made a third of all fresh water _______________. Many people drank this and died.
The Fourth Trumpet **Revelation 8:12**	The _____________, moon, and stars _______________________ by a third.
The Fifth Trumpet **Revelation 9:1–3**	An angel opened a bottomless pit to release _______________, which could hurt people like _______________.
The Sixth Trumpet **Revelation 9:14–16**	_______________________ horsemen were released to kill a third of the people left on Earth.
The Seventh Trumpet **Revelation 11:15–19**	Voices in heaven declared that the world would become Christ's _______________. The _______________ _______________________ was revealed in heaven.

Despite all these judgments, John sees that most of the people in the world do not repent. Instead, they rebel even more against God.

32-C The Antichrist

During the Tribulation, God will allow Satan to work through someone called the **Antichrist**. He will lead the nations of the world in rebellion against God. Other people have been antichrists throughout history, but this person will be the most powerful.

▶ Read **1 John 2:22–23**. How does John describe an antichrist?

____

____

____

▶ The prophet Daniel learned about a few antichrists in his visions. Read **Daniel 8:23–25**. How does Daniel describe this king? What does the king do?

____

____

____

▶ Read **2 Thessalonians 2:1–12** and answer the following questions.

⊙ Paul writes about someone who will rise up against God before the Day of the Lord. How does Paul describe him? (v. 3)

____

____

⊙ What will this man do? (v. 4)

____

____

⊙ How will God eventually defeat him? (v. 8)

____

⊙ But in the meantime, how will the Antichrist deceive people? (v. 9)

____

____

⊙ What will God do to those followers? (vv. 10–11)

____

____

The Seven Bowls

After the judgments of the seals and the trumpets, the sin in the world grows even worse. In Revelation 13, John describes how Satan's servants persecute anyone who chooses to believe in Christ. The Antichrist seems to take over the entire world. He deceives people through many miracles and forces them to bear a mark of loyalty.

► Then John saw the worst judgments of all. Read the passages and use the words below to fill in the blanks.

blood	darkness	Euphrates	hailstones
repent	sea	sores	sun

The First Bowl Revelation 16:2	People got terrible, painful __________________.
The Second Bowl Revelation 16:3	The _______________ turned to blood, and everything in it died.
The Third Bowl Revelation 16:4–7	Rivers and other fresh water became _________________.
The Fourth Bowl Revelation 16:8–9	The _______________ scorched people, but they blasphemed God's name and refused to _________________.
The Fifth Bowl Revelation 16:10–11	The kingdom of those opposing God fell into _________________. People gnawed on their tongues and continued to curse God.
The Sixth Bowl Revelation 16:12	The river ______________________ dried up.
The Seventh Bowl Revelation 16:17–21	A terrible earthquake tore the world apart. The great cities fell along with islands and mountains. Great ___________________ fell.

Winning Your Race

► Read **Matthew 24:42–44** and **2 Peter 3:11–14**. God's judgment will not hurt believers, but how should we wait for Christ's return?

____

____

____

____

The Reign of Christ

Vocabulary

- **Armageddon** – Greek for "hill of Megiddo"; in Scripture, the place where Christ destroys the armies that have gathered against Him

- **Millennium** – One thousand years; in Scripture, a time when Christ reigns physically on Earth

33-A The Patience of God

It can be terrible to read about the judgments and suffering in Revelation. But as much as God hates sin, He loves His children. He judges the world only after many patient warnings. He wants everyone to turn back to Him.

▶ Read the following passages and answer the questions.

⊙ **Exodus 34:6** – How does God describe Himself here?

____

____

____

⊙ **2 Chronicles 30:9** – How will God treat us if we return to Him?

____

____

⊙ **Psalm 33:5** – What does God love?

____

⊙ **1 Timothy 1:16** – Before Paul trusted Christ, he persecuted many believers. What did Christ show by giving Paul mercy?

____

____

⊙ **2 Peter 3:9** – You might remember this verse from Lesson 29. Why does God wait so long to punish wicked people?

____

____

▶ Do you think that God could truthfully call Himself loving if He allowed sin to continue forever? Why or why not?

____

____

____

____

____

▶ We still live in a world where many wicked people seem very powerful. Read **Psalm 37:1–9**. Explain briefly what believers *should* and *should not* do while waiting for Christ to make things right.

____

____

____

33-B Armageddon

After the Tribulation judgments, Christ will end the suffering by coming back to Earth and destroying all the governments and powers that have allied against Him. The Apostle John saw this event happen in a place called **Armageddon**.

▶ Read **Revelation 19:11–21** and mark the best ending to each sentence.

Verse 11 – Here Jesus is called Faithful and True. John describes Him as a . . .

| ☐ Lamb that was slain. | ☐ Rider on a white horse. | ☐ King on His throne. |

Verse 13 – Jesus' robe is dipped in blood, and His name is called . . .

| ☐ the Word of God. | ☐ the Anointed One. | ☐ the Lamb. |

Verse 14 – Following Jesus, clothed in white, are the . . .

| ☐ armies of heaven. | ☐ priests of ancient Israel. | ☐ original disciples. |

Verse 15 – Jesus' sword somehow comes out of His . . .

| ☐ right hand. | ☐ mouth. | ☐ horse. |

<table>
<tr><td colspan="3" style="background:#3d9b95;color:#fff">Verse 16 – As Jesus rides, He bears the title . . .</td></tr>
<tr><td>☐ Messiah.</td><td>☐ Savior of Humanity.</td><td>☐ King of Kings and Lord of Lords.</td></tr>
</table>

<table>
<tr><td colspan="3" style="background:#3d9b95;color:#fff">Verse 19 – Gathered against Jesus were the Beast and . . .</td></tr>
<tr><td>☐ the horsemen of Death.</td><td>☐ all Satan's demons.</td><td>☐ the kings of the earth, with their armies.</td></tr>
</table>

<table>
<tr><td colspan="3" style="background:#3d9b95;color:#fff">Verse 20 – The Beast and false prophet were captured, and the rest were . . .</td></tr>
<tr><td>☐ killed by the sword from Jesus' mouth.</td><td>☐ banished to the ends of the world.</td><td>☐ thrown into the lake of fire.</td></tr>
</table>

▶ Read **Revelation 20:1–3**. At this point, what did John see happen to Satan?

____

____

33-C A Peaceful Reign

With Satan and God's enemies defeated, John now sees Jesus build a physical kingdom on Earth. Many Christians call this time the **Millennium**.

▶ Read **Revelation 20:4** and answer the following questions.

⊙ Who will now reign with Christ?

____

____

⊙ How long will this period last? _______________________________

Many Old Testament prophets described what the Messiah's kingdom on Earth would look like. When Jesus' disciples wanted Him to become a king, they were thinking about this physical kingdom.

▶ Read **Jeremiah 23:5**. How will David's descendant rule as king?

____

____

▶ Read **Isaiah 2:2–4** and answer the following questions.

⊙ Why will many people go to God's temple? (vv. 2–3)

____

____

⦿ As God serves as Judge for the nations, what will people do with their weapons? (v. 4)

____

____

► Read about the Messiah's reign in **Isaiah 65:17–25**. List the three prophecies that most excite you for this kingdom.

⦿ ____

____

⦿ ____

____

⦿ ____

____

Winning Your Race

► Think about how Christ revealed Himself in the Book of Revelation. List five words describing Him.

____

____

LESSON 34
The Final Victory

Vocabulary

- **The Book of Life** – God's record of everyone redeemed by Jesus Christ

34-A The End of Satan

► Look all the way back in **Genesis 3:14–15**. What did God promise that the woman's descendant would do to the serpent?

____

► John saw the final fulfillment of this prophecy. Read **Revelation 20:7–10** and answer the following questions.

⊙ After one thousand years of Christ's reign, what will happen to Satan? (v. 7)

____

⊙ What will he do next? What is his plan? (v. 8)

____

____

⊙ Will he succeed? (v. 9) ☐ Yes ☐ No

⊙ Where will he be thrown forever? (v. 10) _______________________________

Jesus felt the "bite" of the serpent when He suffered and died. But He overcame the power of death by rising again. And at the end, God will crush the serpent's head, finishing him for good.

► When Satan is cast away forever, all his evil is banished with him. Read the following passage and write what will end with Satan.

John 8:44	
2 Corinthians 4:4	
Hebrews 2:14	
Revelation 12:9	

34-B The Great White Throne

After Satan is thrown into the lake of fire, God will judge those who have died. This will be His final judgment over all those who have not yet stood before Christ.

► Read **Revelation 20:11–15** and complete the following summaries.

Verse 11	John saw a _______________________________________, and nothing could hide from the One seated there.
Verses 12–13	All the _______________ stood before the throne to be judged. *The Book of Life* was opened, as were other books that recorded the people's works. The _______________ gave up the dead in it, as did Death and _______________. All people were judged by their deeds.
Verse 14	Then _______________ and _______________ were thrown into the lake of fire. This is called the "second death."
Verse 15	And if anyone's name was not found in the _______________, that person was also thrown into the lake of fire.

► Note **Philippians 4:3** and **Revelation 3:5**. Whose names are in the Book of Life?

____

34-C Visions of Eternity

In the end, God will create a new heaven and earth. He will fill them with beautiful things, but the most wonderful part will be His own presence.

▶ What will forever look like? Read **Revelation 21:1–8** and answer the following:

⊚ Again, where will God live? (v. 3)

____

⊚ How will this new creation be different than the old one? (v. 4)

____

____

⊚ What did God say about the words that John would write down? (v. 5)

____

⊚ What blessing will God give believers? (v. 7)

____

____

⊚ What will wicked people inherit? (v. 8)

____

▶ Finally, read **Revelation 22:16–21**. In your own words, how do you think Jesus wants people to respond to this book?

____

____

____

____

Winning Your Race

▶ Imagine that you arrive in heaven and finally see Jesus face to face.

⊚ How do you think you might feel?

____

____

⊚ What would you want to say to Jesus?

____

____

- ⊙ What would you think about your past life?

____

____

____

▶ Read the following passages:

- ⊙ **John 3:36**

- ⊙ **Romans 8:38–39**

- ⊙ **Philippians 1:6**

- ⊙ **1 John 1:9**

▶ Do you believe your name is written in the Book of Life?　☐ Yes　☐ No

Why or why not?

____

____

____

____

____

____

____

LESSON 35
Review

35-A Reviewing Units 1–5

Unit 1: Preparation

► Write the letter of the best answer. For help, check the page numbers.

1. The Bible includes ___ books. (pp. 5–6)

A. 34	**B.** 100	**C.** 66

2. In Psalm 119, the writer compares the Bible to a light because it ___. (p. 11)

   A. guides our path
   B. keeps us from seeing darkness
   C. runs on Spirit power
   D. All of the above

3. When God's Word was found after being lost for so long, Josiah ___. (pp. 13–14)

   A. renewed Israel's covenant with God
   B. felt distressed and mourned
   C. read it to the people of Israel
   D. All of the above

4. When God called Moses to lead Israel out of Egypt, Moses ___. (p. 16)

   A. fled on a ship headed as far away as possible
   B. made excuses, but finally went
   C. said he would go, but never did
   D. obeyed without hesitation or doubt

5. After seeing Nineveh repent, Jonah was ___. (p. 17)

A. happy	**B.** worried	**C.** angry

6. God delivered Israel from the Midianites through the judge ___. (pp. 23–24)

| **A.** Samson | **B.** Deborah | **C.** Gideon |

7. What is God's ultimate purpose for every believer? (pp. 25–27)

A. to be happy
B. to show others that we obey every command in Scripture
C. to glorify God by being like Christ

8. Which is *not* a sign that believers are filled with the Holy Spirit? (p. 30)

A. singing and worshiping with other believers
B. giving thanks to God
C. submitting to one another
D. being successful in every effort

9. When we worship God, our ___ matters more than anything else. (p. 35)

| **A.** heart | **B.** voice | **C.** appearance |

10. In 1 John 1:9, we read that if we confess our sin to God, He will ___. (p. 39)

A. forgive and cleanse us
B. punish us for telling Him
C. send the Holy Spirit again

Unit 3: The Path

► Mark each statement as true or false.

11. In Exodus 20:12, God commanded children to offer sacrifices for their parents. (p. 48) ☐ True ☐ False

12. Absalom responded badly to his father's failures, but Jonathan did right despite his father's failures. (pp. 53–57) ☐ True ☐ False

13. In Matthew 15:16–20, Jesus explained that our sinful actions come from evil spirits. (pp. 58–59) ☐ True ☐ False

14. John the Baptist prepared the way for Jesus by telling people to repent. (p. 65) ☐ True ☐ False

15. In John 15:1–8, Jesus said that every branch which did not produce fruit would stay on the vine. (p. 66) ☐ True ☐ False

Unit 4: Weights and Distractions

▶ Choose the best answer to finish each sentence.

	16. Ahab was a ___ because he refused to listen to God and His prophet, Elijah. (pp. 71–73)	**A.** body
	17. To ___ means to want something for yourself that belongs to another. (p. 75)	**B.** covet
	18. The ___ is a term in Scripture for our natural desire to sin. (p. 81)	**C.** faith
	19. ___ tempts us to sin by questioning God's truth. (pp. 84–87)	**D.** flesh
	20. The shield of ___ is part of the armor of God, which helps us stand strong against Satan's attacks. (p. 91)	**E.** fool
	21. Jesus said that His disciples would be known by their ___ for each other. (p. 93)	**F.** love
	22. Paul compared the Church to a ___ made from many different but equally useful parts. (p. 101)	**G.** Satan

Unit 5: The Goal

	23. Isaiah described the Messiah as a sacrificial ___, an offering for sin. (p. 106)	**A.** lamb
	24. Hebrews says that Christ is superior to any Old Testament ___. (p. 107)	**B.** living
	25. Jesus told the Samaritan woman that He could give her ___ water. (p. 114)	**C.** priest or sacrifice
	26. In the Beatitudes, Jesus blessed those that hunger and thirst after ___. (p. 119)	**D.** righteousness
	27. Jesus prayed for the Father to remove the "cup" of suffering and death, but He chose to ___ to the Father's will. (p. 124)	**E.** submit
	28. On the ___ day after the crucifixion, Jesus rose again. (p. 128)	**F.** third
	29. In the Great Commission, Jesus said His followers would be ___ all over the world. (pp. 130–131)	**G.** witnesses

35-B Vocabulary

► Write the correct vocabulary word for each definition. If you forget a word, check the page number.

Across

1. To use water to symbolize someone's new relationship with God (p. 63)

3. An Old Testament name for local false gods; can mean "lord" or "ruler" (p. 20)

7. A student or follower who learns from a teacher (p. 25)

9. The event in which one rises upward; in Scripture, Jesus' rise from Earth to heaven (p. 128)

11. A disaster for a large number of people; in Scripture, often reveals God's judgment (p. 103)

12. The practice of worshiping idols or false gods (p. 10)

14. Choosing not to eat, often to focus on praying or some other spiritual activity (p. 75)

16. Greek for "hill of Megiddo"; in Scripture, the place where Christ destroys the armies that have gathered against Him (p. 157)

20. Great suffering, hardship, or trouble (p. 141)

22. To continually oppress or mistreat people, often for their religion or ethnicity (p. 58)

23. To make holy or sacred; to set apart for a special purpose (p. 25)

24. A term for someone who is not Jewish (p. 113)

Down

2. Something that is hated, disgusting, or detestable (p. 58)

4. A "sent one"; a witness of the resurrection of Jesus (p. 128)

5. A wise saying; a short statement that teaches a general principle (p. 71)

6. To grab or take away; a name for the event in which Christ takes believers to be with Him in heaven (p. 146)

8. A story that pictures or illustrates a lesson (p. 15)

10. A method of execution; killing someone by attaching them to an upright piece of wood and leaving them to die (p. 123)

13. A promise or record; the name for the two major divisions of books in the Bible (p. 5)

15. A Jewish holiday celebrating the day God rescued the Israelites from Egypt (p. 103)

17. Someone killed for their religious beliefs (p. 151)

18. A gathering place for Jews to learn and worship (p. 108)

19. A divinely-caused event that does not follow the laws of nature (p. 108)

21. The way God worked through human writers to record Scripture; "God-breathed" (p. 10)

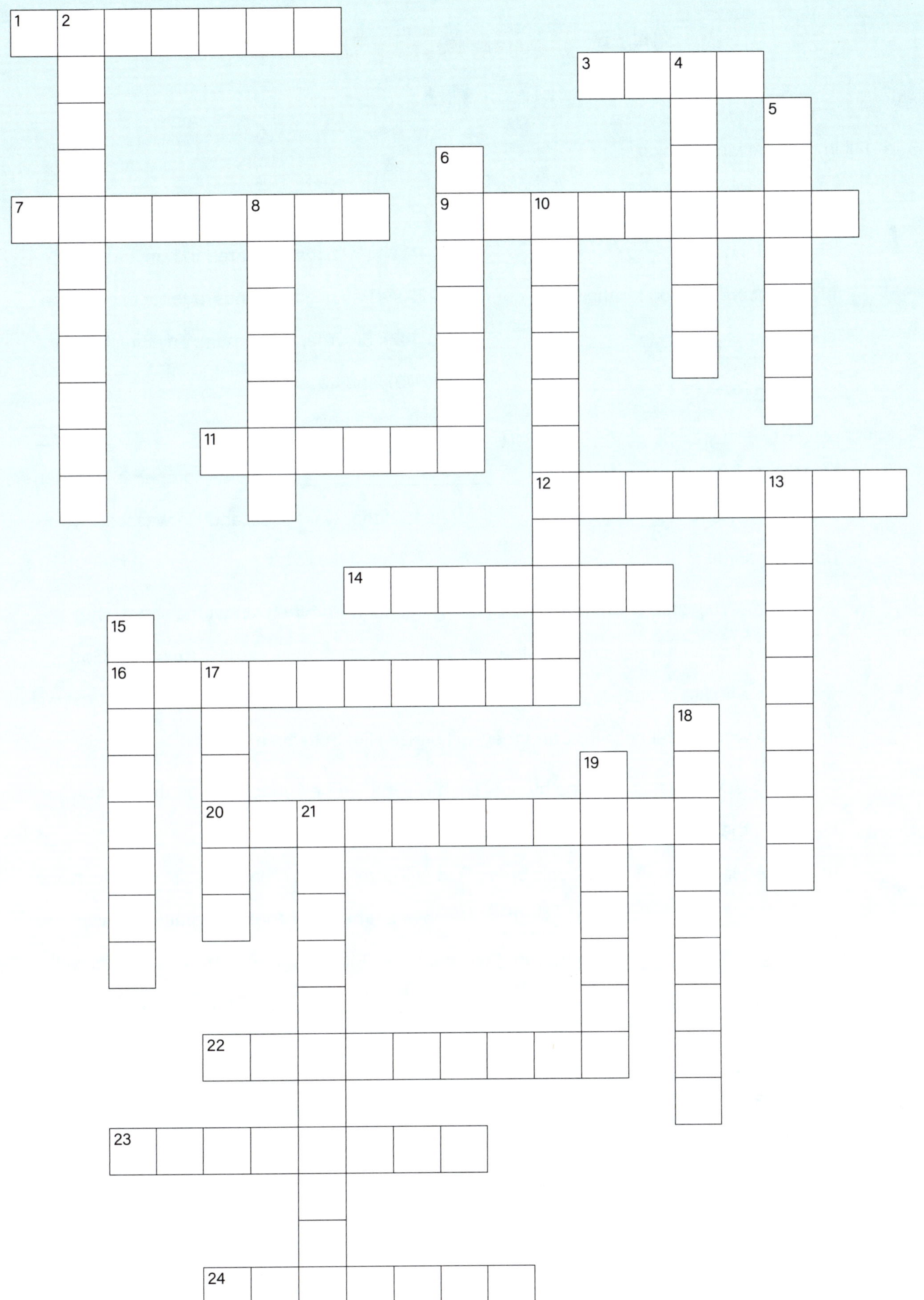

Unit 6: The Prize

▶ Fill in the following blanks.

The Book of Revelation was written by the Apostle _______________ (p. 137). He was on the island of _______________ (p. 137) when Jesus appeared to him and told him to record a vision for the seven churches in Asia. Jesus gave a message for each of the churches: _______________ (p. 142), Smyrna, Pergamum, Thyatira, Sardis, _______________ (p. 143), and Laodicea.

John saw a vision of God on His throne, holding a scroll with seven _______________ (p. 149). At first, no one was found _______________ (p. 149) to open it. But then John saw a slain _______________ (p. 150) that was Jesus, and He was worthy to open the scroll.

When Jesus returns for His Church, He will descend from heaven with a shout, with the voice of an archangel, and with the _______________ (p. 146) of God. Believers who are already _______________ (p. 146) will be raised up first. Christ will judge the works of all believers, and they will praise Him in heaven.

As the seven seals open one by one, each will mark a new judgment on the world. This will begin the period of seven years called the _______________ (p. 153). After the last of these seals open, God will command seven angels to sound seven _______________ (p. 154) one at a time. After these judgments, seven _______________ (p. 156) will pour out God's judgment on the world, as well. During this time, the _______________ (p. 155) will lead people to oppose God.

At the end of seven years, Christ will appear, riding a _______________ (p. 158) horse and leading the armies of heaven to Armageddon. The Beast and the false prophet will be thrown into the lake of fire. Christ will defeat their armies with the _______________ (p. 159) coming from His mouth. Satan will then be bound up in the bottomless pit for

__________________________________ (p. 159) years. After this time, he will be freed for one last

rebellion, but God will throw him into the __________________________________ (p. 161).

After seeing all this, John had a vision of God on a great white __________________________

(p. 162), where He judged all the dead. He judged them by their actions and checked if their

names were written in the Book of __________________ (p. 162). Anyone whose name was

not found there was thrown into the lake of fire.

Then John saw a new __________________________ and __________________________ (p. 163).

Under God's eternal rule, there will be no sorrow, crying, or pain. In the new Jerusalem, there

will be no temple, nor any need for a __________________ or __________________ (p. 140).

God will dwell there with His children.

Hymn Lyrics

It Is Well with My Soul

Verse 1   When peace, like a river, attendeth my way,
When sorrows like sea-billows roll,
Whatever my lot, Thou hast taught me to say,
It is well, it is well with my soul.

Refrain   It is well with my soul,
It is well, it is well with my soul.

Verse 2   Though Satan should buffet, though trials should come,
Let this blest assurance control,
That Christ has regarded my helpless estate,
And hath shed His own blood for my soul.

Verse 3   My sin—oh, the bliss of this glorious thought—
My sin—not in part, but the whole,
Is nailed to the cross and I bear it no more,
Praise the Lord, praise the Lord, O my soul!

Verse 4   And, Lord, haste the day when the faith shall be sight,
The clouds be rolled back as a scroll,
The trump shall resound and the Lord shall descend,
Even so, it is well with my soul.

By Horatio Spafford (1873).

What Wondrous Love

Verse 1
What wondrous love is this,
O my soul, O my soul,
What wondrous love is this,
O my soul:
What wondrous love is this,
That caused the Lord of bliss,
To bear the dreadful curse,
For my soul, for my soul,
To bear the dreadful curse,
For my soul.

Verse 2
When I was sinking down,
Sinking down, sinking down
When I was sinking down,
Sinking down;
When I was sinking down,
Beneath God's righteous frown,
Christ laid aside his crown,
For my soul, for my soul;
Christ laid aside his crown,
For my soul.

Verse 3
To God, and to the Lamb,
I will sing, I will sing,
To God, and to the Lamb,
I will sing,
To God, and to the Lamb,
And the great I AM,
While millions join the theme,
I will sing, I will sing,
While millions join the theme,
I will sing.

By unknown author (early 1800s).

To Be a Pilgrim

Verse 1

He who would valiant be
Against all disaster,
Let him in constancy
Follow the Master
There's no discouragement
Shall make him once relent
His first avowed intent
To be a pilgrim.

Verse 2

Who so beset him round
With dismal stories,
Do but themselves confound,
His strength the more is,
No foes shall stay his might,
Though he with giants fight;
He will make good his right
To be a pilgrim.

Verse 3

Since, Lord, Thou dost defend
Us with Thy Spirit,
We know we at the end
Shall life inherit.
Then fancies flee away!
I'll fear not what men say,
I'll labor night and day
To be a pilgrim.

By John Bunyan (1684).

Now Thank We All Our God

Verse 1
Now thank we all our God,
With heart and hands and voices,
Who wondrous things hath done,
In Whom His world rejoices;
Who from our mother's arms
Has blessed us on our way
With countless gifts of love,
And still is ours today.

Verse 2
O may this bounteous God,
Through all our life be near us,
With ever joyful hearts,
And blessed peace to cheer us;
And keep us in His grace,
And guide us when perplexed,
And free us from all ills,
In this world and the next.

Verse 3
All praise and thanks to God
The Father now be given,
The Son and Him who reigns
With Them in highest heaven;
The one eternal God,
Whom earth and heaven adore;
For thus it was, is now,
And shall be evermore!

By Martin Rinkart (1636).
Translated by Catherine Winkworth.

The Church's One Foundation

Verse 1

The Church's one Foundation
Is Jesus Christ her Lord;
She is His new creation
By water and the word:
From heaven He came and sought her
To be His holy Bride;
With His own blood He bought her,
And for her life He died.

Verse 2

Elect from every nation,
Yet one o'er all the earth,
Her charter of salvation
One Lord, one faith, one birth;
One Holy Name she blesses,
Partakes one holy food,
And to one hope she presses,
With every grace endued.

By Samuel John Stone (1866).

Verse 3

Though with a scornful wonder
Men see her sore oppressed,
By schisms rent asunder,
By heresies distressed,
Yet saints their watch are keeping,
Their cry goes up, "How long?"
And soon the night of weeping
Shall be the morn of song.

Verse 4

'Mid toil and tribulation,
And tumult of her war,
She waits the consummation
Of peace for evermore;
Till with the vision glorious
Her longing eyes are blest,
And the great Church victorious
Shall be the Church at rest.

O the Deep Deep Love of Jesus

Verse 1

O the deep, deep love of Jesus,
Vast, unmeasured, boundless, free!
Rolling as a mighty ocean
In its fullness over me!
Underneath me, all around me,
Is the current of Thy love
Leading onward, leading homeward
To my glorious rest above!

Verse 2

O the deep, deep love of Jesus,
Spread His praise from shore to shore!
How He loveth, ever loveth,
Changeth never, nevermore!
How He watches o'er His loved ones,
Died to call them all His own;
How for them He intercedeth,
Watcheth o'er them from the throne!

Verse 3

O the deep, deep love of Jesus,
Love of every love the best!
'Tis an ocean vast of blessing,
'Tis a haven sweet of rest!
O the deep, deep love of Jesus,
'Tis a heaven of heavens to me;
And it lifts me up to glory,
For it lifts me up to Thee!

By Samuel Trevor Francis (1873).

There Is a Fountain

Verse 1

There is a fountain filled with blood
Drawn from Immanuel's veins;
And sinners plunged beneath that flood
Lose all their guilty stains.

Lose all their guilty stains,
Lose all their guilty stains,
And sinners plunged beneath that flood
Lose all their guilty stains.

Verse 2

The dying thief rejoiced to see
That fountain in his day;
And there may I, as vile as he,
Wash all my sins away.

Wash all my sins away,
Wash all my sins away,
And there may I, as vile as he,
Wash all my sins away.

Verse 3

Dear dying Lamb, Thy precious blood
Shall never lose its power,
Till all the ransomed Church of God
Be saved to sin no more.

Be saved to sin no more,
Be saved to sin no more,
Till all the ransomed Church of God
Be saved to sin no more.

Verse 4

Ever since, by faith, I saw the stream
Thy flowing wounds supply,
Redeeming love has been my theme,
And shall be till I die.

And shall be till I die,
And shall be till I die,
Redeeming love has been my theme,
And shall be till I die.

Verse 5

When this poor lisping, stamm'ring tongue
Lies silent in the grave,
Then in a nobler, sweeter song,
I'll sing Thy power to save.

I'll sing Thy power to save,
I'll sing Thy power to save,
Then in a nobler, sweeter song,
I'll sing Thy power to save.

By William Cowper (1772).

All Creatures of Our God and King

Verse 1 All creatures of our God and King,
Lift up your voice and with us sing
Alleluia, Alleluia!
Thou burning sun with golden beam,
Thou silver moon with softer gleam,
O praise Him, O praise Him,
Alleluia, Alleluia, Alleluia!

Verse 2 Thou rushing wind that art so strong,
Ye clouds that sail in heaven along,
O praise Him, Alleluia!
Thou rising morn in praise rejoice,
Ye lights of evening, find a voice,
O praise Him, O praise Him,
Alleluia, Alleluia, Alleluia!

Verse 3 Thou flowing water, pure and clear,
Make music for thy Lord to hear,
Alleluia, Alleluia!
Thou fire so masterful and bright,
That givest man both warmth and light,
O praise Him, O praise Him,
Alleluia, Alleluia, Alleluia!

Verse 4 Let all things their Creator bless,
And worship Him in humbleness,
O praise Him, Alleluia!
Praise, praise the Father, praise the Son,
And praise the Spirit, Three in One.
O praise Him, O praise Him,
Alleluia, Alleluia, Alleluia!

Original poem by St. Francis of Assisi (early 1200s).
Hymn by William Henry Draper.

O For a Thousand Tongues to Sing

Verse 1

O for a thousand tongues to sing
My great Redeemer's praise,
The glories of my God and King,
The triumphs of His grace!

Verse 2

My gracious Master and my God,
Assist me to proclaim,
To spread through all the earth abroad
The honors of Thy name.

Verse 3

Jesus! the name that charms our fears,
That bids our sorrows cease,
'Tis music in the sinner's ears,
'Tis life, and health, and peace.

Verse 4

He breaks the power of canceled sin,
He sets the prisoner free,
His blood can make the foulest clean,
His blood availed for me.

By Charles Wesley (1739).

O Little Town of Bethlehem

Verse 1

O little town of Bethlehem!
How still we see thee lie;
Above thy deep and dreamless sleep
The silent stars go by;
Yet in thy dark streets shineth
The everlasting Light;
The hopes and fears of all the years
Are met in thee tonight.

Verse 2

For Christ is born of Mary,
And gathered all above,
While mortals sleep, the angels keep
Their watch of wondering love.
O morning stars, together
Proclaim the holy birth!
And praises sing to God the King
And peace to men on earth.

By Phillips Brooks (1868).

Verse 3

How silently, how silently,
The wondrous gift is given!
So God imparts to human hearts
The blessings of His heaven.
No ear may hear His coming,
But in this world of sin,
Where meek souls will receive Him still,
The dear Christ enters in.

Verse 4

O holy Child of Bethlehem!
Descend to us, we pray;
Cast out our sin, and enter in,
Be born in us to-day.
We hear the Christian angels
The great glad tidings tell;
O come to us, abide with us,
Our Lord Immanuel!

Vocabulary

A

Abomination – Something that is hated, disgusting, or detestable (p. 58)

Abound – To increase, fill, and overflow (p. 25)

Alpha and Omega – The first and last letters of the Greek alphabet; in the Book of Revelation, a phrase referring to God's power over all things, beginning to end (p. 137)

Ambassador – A messenger or representative; someone who represents another (p. 93)

Antichrist – Someone who is against Jesus Christ (p. 151)

Apostle – A "sent one"; a witness of the resurrection of Jesus (p. 128)

Archangel – An angel appointed over a special task; a chief angel (p. 146)

Ark of the Covenant – A gold-plated chest containing important items from Israel's history, including the Ten Commandments; a symbol of God's presence with His people (p. 48)

Armageddon – Greek for "hill of Megiddo"; in Scripture, the place where Christ destroys the armies that have gathered against Him (p. 157)

Ascension – The event in which one rises upward; in Scripture, Jesus' rise from Earth to heaven (p. 128)

Atonement – When something wrong is erased or canceled (p. 5)

B

Ba'al – An Old Testament name for many local false gods; can mean "lord" or "ruler" (p. 20)

Baptize – To use water to symbolize someone's new relationship with God (p. 63)

The Beatitudes – Eight "blessings" that begin Jesus' Sermon on the Mount (p. 118)

Beelzebub / Beelzebul – A name used in Scripture to refer to Satan or another demon (p. 67)

Bitterness – Hating someone for past wrongdoing; rehearsing someone's faults in your mind (p. 38)

Blasphemy – Insulting God or something sacred; saying something untrue about God (p. 123)

Blessed – Having special favor, grace, or happiness (p. 118)

The Book of Life – God's record of everyone redeemed by Jesus Christ (p. 161)

C

Carnal – Relating to physical desires and appetites; often relating to sinful pleasure (p. 79)

Censer – A bowl or container for burning incense (p. 151)

Centurion – A Roman military officer; traditionally commanded 100 soldiers, but often more (p. 108)

Chaff – The empty husks left behind after threshing grain; the useless part of the plant (p. 43)

Commandment – A law or rule; in Exodus, the Ten Commandments begin God's Law (p. 48)

Confess – To admit wrongdoing; to reveal what you believe (p. 38)

Conform – To become like something or someone (p. 25)

Conscience – Inner feelings of right or wrong; our moral sense (p. 98)

Contentment – Peace and gratitude for what we already have; happiness in our current state (p. 75)

The Council / Sanhedrin – A group of Jewish leaders who made legal and religious decisions for the people (p. 123)

Covenant – A binding agreement between two or more people; a promise (p. 10)

Crucifixion – A method of execution; killing someone by attaching them to an upright piece of wood and leaving them to die (p. 123)

 **D**

The Day of the Lord – In Scripture, a time when God fulfills His promises in an undeniable way (p. 151)

Deceit – Lying; making a false statement (p. 38)

Defile – To corrupt; to make unholy or impure (p. 58)

Devil – Another name for Satan; means "liar" or "deceiver" (p. 79)

Disciple – A student or follower who learns from a teacher (p. 25)

Doctrine – An important teaching or belief, often by a religious group (p. 10)

Doubt – To distrust; a feeling of uncertainty or unbelief about something (p. 15)

E

The Elect – In Scripture, another term for Christians; people chosen by God (p. 151)

Envy / Coveting – Wanting something that another person has, even if it's sinful to take (p. 75)

Epistle – A letter; one of the 21 letters in the New Testament (p. 5)

Exalt – To lift higher; to call attention to (p. 25)

F

The Fall – Humanity's turn from God toward sin and death; the results of the first sin (p. 84)

Famine – A time when many people have very little food (p. 151)

Fasting – Choosing not to eat, often to focus on praying or some other spiritual activity (p. 75)

Favor – Special blessings or grace; goodwill (p. 34)

Firstborn – The first child of a husband and wife (p. 53)

Fleece – A coat of wool; often taken from sheep (p. 20)

The Flesh – The part of us that wants to sin; our mortal weakness (p. 29)

Foolishness – Refusing to learn; using knowledge poorly; the opposite of wisdom (p. 71)

Foreknowledge – To know something ahead of time; to know about an event before it happens (p. 123)

Forerunner – Someone who goes ahead of another, often to prepare the way (p. 63)

Forgive – To not hold people's wrongs or failures against them; to give up revenge (p. 38)

G

Gentile – A term for someone who is not Jewish (p. 113)

Glorify - To give honor and praise to someone; in Scripture, to point toward God's glory (p. 25)

Glory – The honor, praise, or credit for being great (p. 20)

Gospel – "Good news" or teaching about Jesus (p. 5)

The Great Commission – The task Jesus gave His followers to make more disciples for Him (p. 128)

Greed – A desire for more than what is good or needed; the opposite of gratitude (p. 75)

H

Hallowed – Set apart as special, sacred, or holy (p. 118)

The Heart – Used in Scripture to mean our deepest beliefs and attitudes; our core, inner self (p. 58)

Honor – To show great respect or reverence; to value the good in someone (p. 48)

Hypocrite – Someone who pretends to be better than they are; a person who contradicts their words with their actions (p. 58)

I

Idolatry – The practice of worshiping idols or false gods (p. 10)

Iniquity – A wicked or evil action; a sin (p. 103)

Inspiration – The way God worked through human writers to record Scripture; "God-breathed" (p. 10)

J

Justice – The state of being just, lawful, or right; fair punishment for wrongdoing (p. 53)

Justify – To declare that someone is innocent or righteous; to defend something as right (p. 137)

L

Leaven / Yeast – A single-cell fungus used in breadmaking to help the dough rise (p. 98)

Leprosy – In Scripture, a term to describe diseases that could result in sores, loss of feeling, and deformities; was once untreatable (p. 108)

M

Magistrate – A government official that helps apply and enforce the law (p. 29)

Malice – The desire to harm someone; hurtful thoughts (p. 38)

Manna – A bread-like food that God gave Israel in the wilderness (p. 84)

Martyr – Someone killed for their religious beliefs (p. 151)

Meditate – To think deeply and continually about something (p. 43)

Millennium – One thousand years; in Scripture, a time when Christ reigns physically on Earth (p. 157)

Miracle – A divinely-caused event that does not follow the laws of nature (p. 108)

O

Obey – To do what someone else says to do; to comply or submit your will to another (p. 48)

P

Pagan – Relating to a religion that worships many gods or even nature itself (p. 103)

Parable – A story that pictures or illustrates a lesson (p. 15)

Passover – A Jewish holiday celebrating the day God rescued the Israelites from Egypt (p. 103)

Peacemaker – A person who ends conflict in a lasting way (p. 118)

Pentecost – The "fiftieth day" after Easter; when the Spirit first arrived to bless the Church (p. 132)

Persecute – To continually oppress or mistreat people, often for their religion or ethnicity (p. 58)

Pharisees – A Jewish religious group that added their own rules to God's law (p. 58)

Plague – A disaster for a large number of people; in Scripture, often reveals God's judgment (p. 103)

Prophet – Someone who shares a spiritual message (p. 5)

Propitiation – The act of propitiating; avoiding God's judgment for sin by offering a sacrifice (p. 103)

Proverb – A wise saying; a short statement that teaches a general principle (p. 71)

R

Rapture – To grab or take away; a name for the event in which Christ takes believers to be with Him in heaven (p. 146)

Rebel – To oppose a ruler or some other authority, often with hatred or violence (p. 53)

Reconciliation – The act of reconciling; restoring a good relationship (p. 93)

Rejoice – To take joy from something good; in Scripture, to appreciate God's gifts (p. 34)

Repent – To regret sin and turn back toward God; to ask God to forgive you (p. 38)

Reproof / Rebuke – To tell people that they have done wrong (p. 10)

Resurrection – The event in which someone dead becomes alive again (p. 128)

Revelation – Something that is revealed or shown; God's communication to us (p. 15)

S

Sackcloth – Rough fabric used for sacks or bags; in Scripture, often worn to show sadness (p. 75)

Saint – A sacred or holy person; in Scripture, a term for a believer or Christian (p. 146)

Samaritan – In Jesus' time, a person from Samaria who descended from both Jews and Gentiles (p. 113)

Sanctify – To make holy or sacred; to set apart for a special purpose (p. 25)

Satan – An evil being opposed to God and those who follow Him; means "adversary" (p. 79)

Scourge / Flog – To beat or lash with a whip (p. 123)

Scripture – Sacred writings; another name for the Bible (p. 5)

The Sermon on the Mount – The longest message from Jesus recorded in the Gospels (p. 118)

Sin – Turning away from God; to break God's Law (p. 38)

Sovereignty – Power and authority; in Scripture, God's sole rulership over everything (p. 137)

Stricken – Struck or beaten; suffering under violent abuse (p. 103)

Submit – To serve someone or follow leadership; to put your wants under another's (p. 29)

Synagogue – A gathering place for Jews to learn and worship (p. 108)

T

Tabernacle – In Scripture, a tent compound where God showed His presence to Israel (p. 5)

Temple – A holy or sacred place for worship (p. 93)

Temptation – The act of tempting; any pressure to do wrong; can refer to the thing that tempts (p. 84)

Testament – A promise or record; the name for the two major divisions of books in the Bible (p. 5)

Testimony – A record or witness, often of something important (p. 67)

Thresh – To separate grain from the rest of the plant (p. 20)

Tongues – In the New Testament, a term for different languages (p. 132)

Tradition – A custom that is practiced over a long time; a long-held set of beliefs (p. 58)

Trespass / Transgress – To step over a line or boundary; to break a rule (p. 79)

Tribulation – Great suffering, hardship, or trouble (p. 141)

V

Vineyard – A place for growing grapevines (p. 15)

Vow – A serious, unbreakable promise, sometimes to God Himself (p. 53)

W

Winepress – In ancient times, a hard floor or pit where people squeezed grapes to make wine (p. 20)

Wisdom – The ability to use knowledge well; insight and understanding (p. 10)

The World – In Scripture, can mean the system of power built by those who oppose God (p. 79)

Wormwood – A very bitter herb (p. 151)

Scripture Memory Report Sheet

Name: ______________________________________ **Teacher:** ______________________________

Ls.	Scripture	Due Date	Signature
1	Psalm 119:9–10		
2	Psalm 119:11–12		
3	**Psalm 119:9–12**		
4	Galatians 5:16		
5	Galatians 5:17		
6	**Galatians 5:16–17**		
7	Galatians 5:22–23		
8	**Galatians 5:16–17, 22–23**		
9	Proverbs 3:1–2		
10	Proverbs 3:3–4		
11	**Proverbs 3:1–4**		
12	Proverbs 3:5–6		
13	Proverbs 3:7–8		
14	**Proverbs 3:5–8**		
15	James 1:2–3		
16	James 1:4		
17	James 1:5		
18	**James 1:2–5**		
19	James 1:6		
20	James 1:7–8		
21	**James 1:6–8**		
22	Philippians 2:5–6		
23	Philippians 2:7–8		
24	**Philippians 2:5–8**		
25	Philippians 2:9		
26	Philippians 2:10		
27	Philippians 2:11		
28	**Philippians 2:9–11**		
29	1 Thessalonians 4:13		
30	1 Thessalonians 4:14		
31	1 Thessalonians 4:15		
32	**1 Thessalonians 4:13–15**		
33	1 Thessalonians 4:16		
34	1 Thessalonians 4:17–18		
35	**1 Thessalonians 4:16–18**		